Yet the powers of the soul are far from being confined
to functions that serve the body.
Of what concern is it to the body that you measure
the heavens, gather the number of the stars, determine
the magnitude of each, know what space lies
between them, with what swiftness or slowness they
complete their courses, how many degrees
this way or that they decline? I confess, indeed, that astronomy has
some use; but I am only showing that in this
deepest investigation of heavenly things there is no organic
symmetry, but here is an activity of the soul
distinct from the body. I have put forth one example, from
which it will be easy for my readers to derive the rest.
Manifold indeed is the nimbleness of the soul,
with which it surveys heaven and earth, joins past to future,
retains in memory something heard long before,
nay pictures to itself whatever it pleases. Manifold also is the
skill with which it devises things incredible,
and which is the mother of so many marvelous devices.
These are unfailing signs of divinity in man.

JOHN CALVIN,
Institutes of the Christian Religion

A LITTLE
HANDBOOK
on
HAVING
A SOUL

DAVID HANSEN

InterVarsity Press
Downers Grove, Illinois

© 1997 by David Hansen

All rights reserved. No part of this book may be reproduced in any form without written permission from InterVarsity Press, P.O. Box 1400, Downers Grove, IL 60515.

InterVarsity Press® is the book-publishing division of InterVarsity Christian Fellowship®, a student movement active on campus at hundreds of universities, colleges and schools of nursing in the United States of America, and a member movement of the International Fellowship of Evangelical Students. For information about local and regional activities, write Public Relations Dept., InterVarsity Christian Fellowship, 6400 Schroeder Rd., P.O. Box 7895, Madison, WI 53707-7895.

Cover photograph: Dennis Flaherty

ISBN 0-8308-1679-8

Printed in the United States of America ∞

Library of Congress Cataloging-in-Publication Data

Hansen, David, 1953-
    A little handbook on having a soul/David Hansen.
        p.   cm.
    Includes bibliographical references.
    ISBN 0-8308-1679-8 (alk. paper)
    1. Soul. 2. Spiritual life—Christianity. I. Title.
BT741.2.H36   1997
233'.5—dc21   97-12920
                                                                          CIP

21   20   19   18   17   16   15   14   13   12   11   10   9   8   7   6   5   4   3   2   1

14   13   12   11   10   09   08   07   06   05   04   03   02   01   00   99   98   97

Acknowledgments

The following friends spent many hours reading and correcting various drafts of *A Little Handbook on Having a Soul*. The book is far better for their help. You cannot begin to imagine how many mistakes they helped me to avoid and how their encouragement spurred me on. All errors are mine.

Mike Van Dordrecht, Santa Rosa, California; Bob Coughlin, Belgrade, Montana; Tim Fearer, Oxnard, California; Eric Peterson, Tacoma, Washington; Carol Miles, Bedminster, New Jersey; Steve Mathewson, Dry Creek, Montana; Debbie Hansen, Belgrade, Montana; Luther Nelson, West Yellowstone, Montana; Allan Poole, Durham, North Carolina; Joni Patterson-Croskey, Bozeman, Montana; David Horn, South Hamilton, Massachusetts; Bruce Becker, Philadelphia, Pennsylvania.

Special thanks go to Dave Dooley, Bozeman, Montana, who read the first draft and the copyedited draft. I am supremely grateful to Rodney Clapp, editor at InterVarsity Press, for supporting this project from the beginning, and for his helpful comments on the second draft. I cannot speak enough thanks to my wife Debbie and to our children, Evan, Sarah and Laura, for their liberal gifts of kindness and understanding to me during the many dark days and weeks of writing and rewriting when nothing seemed to be working.

Finally, I wish to dedicate this book to my parents, Jim and Margaret Hansen of Spokane, Washington. They are folks of great soul. My father loves all things natural. My mother loves arts and literature. Both love the gospel. This book is only a frail portrayal of souls as fine as theirs. Whatever may be valuable here I dedicate to them as a token of my respect and my love.

Introduction

The soul is more like a river than a street, more like a forest than a city, and more like a wild trout than a laboratory rat. Thanks be to God. However, most of us live on streets instead of rivers, in cities instead of forests, and nearer to rats than trout. So we mostly write and read in *linear* fashion, that is, corresponding to a straight line. Linear writing follows a logical, somewhat predictable progression from beginning to end.

Style

This book is more like a river than a street. Its course is unpredictable. If when you read you enjoy not knowing what is coming next, if you like picking up clues here and there, if you like books with musing questions some of which are answered later, but many of which are never answered, then you may enjoy this book. If you do not enjoy books like that, don't give up. You may find the reading satisfying, as long as you recognize from the beginning that this book is an exploration, not a lecture.

This book is like a handbook on a river, in which we walk the river together noting its many features. The river itself provides the consistency, the logic of the journey. We follow its course. But rivers are whimsical things, and the closer you get to them, the more unpredictable they become. As we move upstream, side streams and sloughs attract our attention. We notice natural springs entering the current; perhaps some are even hot springs—water flowing through rock that hasn't completely cooled from the last intrusion of magma thousands of years ago. Wildflowers change as we go, as do the trees. Some sections are treeless, others support trees that thrive in dry climate; later, who knows how soon, we may walk into a grove of deliciously dark, heavy cedars. Likewise, the geography of each human soul is varied and unpredictable.

Exploring a river is rigorous. Though you do not walk fast, you are constantly climbing over logs, pushing your way through brush and climbing banks. Walking upstream through rushing water is tough. Simply keeping your balance walking over slippery rocks requires every muscle from your neck down. On the other hand, exploring a river also requires stops to look deeply, smell carefully and touch softly.

At times in this handbook on the soul you will be climbing steep banks or wading upstream through fast water over slick rocks. Then there will be times when you sit in the shade admiring a wild orchid, or in the sun, turning over river rocks, paying your respects to aquatic insects. After sniffing a wild iris in a cedar grove you may be confronted by deep, fast water that must be crossed if you are to continue. If you accept the challenge of fording the stream, the rewards on the other side may be great.

All rivers flow unevenly in different sections. In a day's walk up the rivers I explore in Montana there are sections of heavy, fast water—dangerous really—which pour into slow, deep, glassy water that reflects realities unseen under other circumstances. Then the river widens out into long stretches of shallow "riffles," water from three inches to two feet deep, flowing swiftly over small rocks and gravel.

A river takes bends and then straightens out in what appear to be random patterns. The bends and straights and right angles are all part of the river's character, and part of its life. Trout might survive, but they could never thrive, in a straight river. And we would survive, but we could never thrive, in a world of straight rivers, triangular mountains and forests where leaves fell from trees in neat little stacks all in a row.

Sometimes rivers go underground. You'll be walking downstream and you notice much less water flowing in one section than in the section above it or below it. Occasionally this is an optical illusion: the water is flowing more swiftly and perhaps more deeply than it looks. Sometimes, though, it isn't an illusion: some of the water is seeping downstream through an underground stratum of rock, so part of the river really has disappeared.

Then there is the Salinas River in California, the longest underground river in the world. You follow its course by looking for sand and gravel and lines of trees. The water is there. And it is flowing. But you can't see it.

The soul is like that. At times we can feel our soul as if it were on the very surface of our skin. Great stories draw our souls to the surface of our existence as a haystack draws shy deer into an open field in winter. Great music quivers our souls, just as plucking the fat E string on a guitar jiggles the B string in harmonic vibration. A great sermon makes our soul rise and walk forward to the altar, even if the body stays fast in its seat. Most often, however, we barely sense our soul; it flows quietly and deeply in our life. It is still there: we follow it by looking for signs of its presence.

The truth is, the soul is a lot like the Salinas River. You have to follow it much of the way by signs of water, rather than by seeing the water itself. In this book there are times when the soul goes underground; then all we can do is point to signs of soul.

Reasons

I wander rivers a lot, but never without a purpose. I like to catch trout on a fly. Similarly, I wander intellectually a lot, but never without a purpose. I am a pastor, and I want to lead people to follow Christ. So although this book wanders as it explores, it is not purposeless.

In my pastoral work I have become convinced that many devout Christians have slowly lost their understanding and appreciation for what their soul is and how it operates. Unfortunately, the results of modern biblical scholarship have reinforced the problem. Much of the work has been true and necessary. However, we have not replaced what has been lost with new understandings of what it means to have a soul.

In the twentieth century, conservative and liberal scholarship discovered in biblical language study that the Hebrew word *nephesh* and the Greek word *psyche*, words frequently translated "soul" in the King James Version of the Bible, often do not carry the meaning of the English word *soul.* A good example can be found in Genesis, where the King James Version tells us, "And Abram took Sarai his wife, and Lot his brother's son, and all their substance that they had gathered, and the *souls* that they had gotten in Haran; and they went forth to go into the land of Canaan; and into the land of Canaan they came" (Gen 12:5). The New International Version and the New King James Version translate *nephesh* as "people" instead of "souls," which makes a lot more sense. But the issue goes deeper than simply adjusting our Bible translations.

Bruce Waltke, writing on the word *nephesh* in the *Theological Wordbook of the Old Testament,* published by Moody Press, reflects the general results of modern scholarship, conservative and liberal. He says: "In Gen 2.7 'man became a living creature' *[nephesh]* the substantive must not be taken in the metaphysical, theological sense in which we tend to use the term 'soul.' "[1] The article goes on to say that the Hebrew words for "spirit," "heart" and "image" depict the human being's relation to God.[2] *The Anchor Bible Dictionary,* a work of over six thousand entries, does not contain an article on the biblical doctrine of the soul.[3]

Though scholarship has treated the word *nephesh* rather severely, some correction was long overdue. The church's traditional teachings on the soul—Catholic, Protestant and Orthodox —were heavily influenced by the Greek philosophy of Plato, especially his doctrine of the immortality of the soul, which the church took as gospel from early on. Biblical evidence clearly contradicts the idea of the immortality of the soul. The Bible does not negate the idea that the soul can survive death and live forever. The Bible negates the idea that the soul is, all by itself, natively immortal—that is, that the soul is made of immortal, invisible, immutable stuff that can't be squashed, burned, watered down or in any way destroyed, even by God himself. The Scriptures strongly support the idea that the soul can live forever—but only with God's presence and support, just as we live now.

When scholars saw that the traditional doctrine of the soul was floated by Platonist hot air instead of the Scriptures, they were right to demand a change. But what is the alternative? Studying the Hebrew and Greek words for "soul" doesn't give much help. The prevailing view became that whatever the soul is, soul and body make up one indivisible being. The upshot was the belief that body and soul cannot be understood separately.

There is some real truth to this. But that has not kept us from studying kidneys, nostrils and tendons apart from the soul. Yet it has kept us from studying the soul. So the soul receded into the background. It sank into the body, so to speak, and thus our view of what it means to be human has resigned itself to a definite materialism. Because of this, many pastors and spiritual directors know far more about kidneys, nostrils and tendons than they do about the soul. This intellectual erosion has yielded sad results.

Too many Christians fear that heaven will be boring. Many of us believe that when we die our soul goes to heaven. The problem is, with our understanding of the soul compromised, we may wonder whether anything worth calling human goes to heaven. If the soul is almost nothing, maybe nothing much goes to heaven. If nothing much goes to heaven, maybe nothing much happens in heaven. Maybe heaven is boring, which would make it a lot like hell. On the other hand, if we understand the soul to be our essential human, spiritual self, the cockpit of our experience of all that is true, good, beautiful and holy in this life, then the soul in heaven may be in for quite a ride.

The idea of looking forward to heaven causes some Christians unease; they fear that too often we become "heavenly bound and no earthly good." This fear, though not without basis, may not be as serious a threat to our stewardship of physical life as the unchecked materialism that results from ignoring the soul and life's natural spirituality in this world and in the world to come.

Christians have become greedy. We spend too much on ourselves. We spend too much on our houses and our clothes and our cars and our computers and our vacations and our hobbies. This has always been a problem, but I think it's gotten worse. The sheer size of the homes many Christians feel they "need" these days leaves me with the strong impression that we are not storing up our treasures in heaven. Which I suppose makes sense if heaven isn't expected to be all that great.

There is a perverse logic to the idea that some Christians spend too much on themselves because of an unrealistically spiritual orientation. If the spiritual life is what really matters, then why not spend all you want on yourself? Why should it matter as long as the soul is in good shape? Naturally this affects our concepts of ministry. If our real hope is in heaven, why should we do anything more for the poor than evangelize them? As long as heaven is just, why bother about justice in this terminally goofed-up world? Making sure people get to heaven should be enough.

This mean and unscriptural argument has been used in the past and is still used. It is a heretical perversion of biblical teaching, a form of gnosticism (we'll get to the Gnostics later). Unfortunately, gnosticism hangs on to Christianity like athlete's foot spores to feet: the spores are always there, just waiting for the proper conditions to bloom. The proper conditions for gnosticism are a misunderstanding of the soul and our spiritual nature fed by greed and orneriness.

When modern biblical scholarship demoted the soul, many people thought this was good: if we teach the importance of the body, people will take poverty and social justice more seriously. It makes sense, after all, that if we care more about our own bodies, we will care more about other people's bodies too. Well, it sounded good in theory, but somewhere along the way it dawned on some folks that having a nice cabin at the lake was a pretty important thing for the body, and so was belonging to a health club, and so was comfortable furniture, and so on. In my opinion the idea backfired. We have simply become more materialistic, a tendency consistent with our overphysical view of what it means to be human.

It shouldn't surprise us that our prayer lives went downhill.

In the 1980s Protestant Christians began to notice: "Hey, we don't really know how to pray anymore; who can teach us?" Many of us turned to Roman Catholics, or to Protestant authors who had already been reading Roman Catholics, like Eugene Peterson. I began to visit an old Catholic priest to learn about prayer. Some Protestants just became Roman Catholics.

In my own search I began reading Hans Urs von Balthasar, Baron Friedrich von Hügel and St. John of the Cross, and of course the soul is all over the place in their writings. I expected an emphasis on the soul in von Hügel and St. John of the Cross, but I was surprised to see it throughout von Balthasar's work *Prayer.* He is a modern theologian, a Swiss Roman Catholic, a young contemporary of Karl Barth. At first I figured that his references to the soul were extraneous to his theology. No. The more I read, the more convinced I became that a positive theology of the soul was critical to his thinking. I became more convinced of this as I read sections of his *The Glory of the Lord: A Theological Aesthetics.* It is not a coincidence that von Balthasar has written what some consider the greatest book on the theology of prayer *and* the greatest book on the theology of aesthetics.

It shouldn't surprise us, then, that as we become more materialistic, we become less able to talk about what it means that something is beautiful. Actually our materialism may stem from our failure to understand beauty. Beauty, even in its most physical manifestations, is spiritual. God in his glory is beautiful, and God has made his universe to be a reflection of his glory. When we see something beautiful, the beauty we see is related to the glory of

God, beauty's origin. Beauty has no existence without God. Beauty is a derived spiritual quality inhering in creation. People age and die, paintings get dirty, stars implode. But the fact that beautiful things change over time and lose their beauty never diminishes the reality of beauty. Beauty exists in and with God as a constituent part of God's being—like love.

Isn't that what heaven is about? Prayer, heaven, beauty, social justice. They are all connected. The more I think about it, the more important the soul becomes to my understanding of these essential qualities and the vital connections between them.

The soul needs to be saved. The "salvation of the soul" has fallen into disfavor in this century. It is true that Jesus talked constantly about the need to feed the poor and care for the body. He taught us to pray, "Give us this day our daily bread." Social justice is a major theme throughout the Scriptures. Nevertheless, the effort to come up with some of kind of "salvation of the body" has not produced practical results, unless you consider health clubs, self-help literature and retreat centers with swimming pools major religious progress. It would be interesting for someone to do a study to see whether the church really was more generous in the century of the "salvation of the body" than in previous generations.

The real problem with the concept of the salvation of the body is that the body doesn't need salvation because it was never lost. The idea that the body is lost is another one of those gnostic errors that we will discuss later. The body doesn't need food, clothing, shelter or healing because it is bad or lost. Sin comes from the soul. The soul must be saved, because it is the soul that is lost. The soul is the part of us that revels in good and is addicted to evil. So we cannot talk about the soul without talking about basic Christian salvation.

Plan
This book consists of three distinctly different parts. They are distinct enough that you may wonder if I have written three tracts instead of one book. But then again, if you looked at the Missouri

River where it joins the Mississippi River at St. Louis, and behind the Fort Peck Dam in eastern Montana, and at its headwaters in Yellowstone Park and the Big Hole Valley, you would be tempted to think you were looking at three different rivers. This is a handbook on the soul, and like a handbook on a river, it must have distinctly different parts in order to cover the length and breadth of this topic. The soul is all over the map of what it means to be human, and this book attempts to reflect that fact.

Part one, "The Soul Defined," is a collection of stories and propositions. As the title implies, part one is an attempt to provide some basic definitions, descriptions and distinctions about the human soul. In the book I use stories, metaphors and similes liberally, by necessity. The stories are extended metaphors for the soul. The stories are just as important as the propositions. Stories are a primary source for understanding the soul.

Part two, "The Soul at Work," is a collection of stories. Part two is an attempt to see the soul in action as it is integrated in our whole lives, body and soul, and as we interact with physical and spiritual realities—specifically with beauty, goodness, truth and holiness. Part two is a collection of extended metaphors on the nature of the soul. This section is less demanding to read than the other two, but it is more demanding to interpret, since in this section the reader must provide his or her own propositions. Of course this is the kind of thing the soul does: the soul finds the meaning in our everyday lives. In this section the soul at work is your own soul.

I like the story section because it forces you to work like a pastor. We work at doctoring the soul, and our only access to the soul in the people we work with is their stories. We listen to their stories, think through them, pray through them, and we listen to them through Bible stories. Soul work is story work.

Part three, "The Soul Redeemed," is about the salvation of the soul. In part three we return to the story/proposition style of writing with a more theological bent. I hope part three brings the gospel into fresh words and challenging thinking. Besides edifying those who are already Christians, the evangelist in me hopes that some who are not sure where they stand with Christ will hear a compelling call to enter into Christ's life and death in faith and to follow him in this life and into the next.

Reflections

From the beginning of this project, when it was nothing but daydreams, until now, I have been acutely aware of the fact that I am a pastor writing a book about the soul, and not a theologian, a biblical scholar or a psychologist. And yet, somewhat embarrassingly, this fact has not kept me from making statements as if I were a theologian, a biblical scholar or a psychologist. For that matter, I am not a short-story writer, and yet I have filled my book with short stories. I am a pastor, and as a pastor I am called on in my work to do theology, biblical studies and psychology, and I listen to and tell stories all day long. (Since this is true confession time, I should admit that I am not a professional fly fisherman, and there again, I talk about fly-fishing as if I were an expert.)

Most of us pastors are experts at talking confidently about all kinds of things we know just a little bit about. However, when you put the little bit we know together, it becomes something valuable: sort of like a general contractor who knows just enough about framing and plumbing and electrical work and drywall to organize a construction job and get it done. Knowing a little bit about a lot of things is the only way I can do my job, because the human soul is my everyday work site.

I take it as patently true that no one is an expert in enough stuff to master the soul. As a consequence this book is filled with a little bit of information from a lot of areas and a lot of intuition and speculation. But when your life's work is the cure of souls, and nobody can really tell you how to do it, you have no choice but to listen to soul stories, trying to understand them by pasting together what you hear with bits and pieces of knowledge, intuition and speculation. In some ways this book represents what I do in my average workday. My pastoral work advanced when I began listening to people's stories like rivers instead of like lectures!

And so I invite you to come along. We will follow the banks of the soul. At times we will wade out deep. More than once I have waded out into that large, powerful river, the Yellowstone, thinking I was fording a shallow riffle only to find myself drawn into a deep, heavy flow. When the water reaches the middle of your chest, you feel yourself beginning to float; then the gravel under your feet begins slipping, and the water has you. If I'd figured the water better, I'd have stayed a lot drier over the years.

Getting pulled under is part of wading a river, and I suspect it is part of writing, and probably of reading, a book on the soul. The only good reason to wade out deep, of course, is to catch big fish. Whatever else we accomplish here, I really hope we catch some big fish.

Part 1

The Soul
Defined

••

One

The Soul
Is What Goes
to Heaven

•••

*I*n Montana people heal grief with Jell-O salads. It's as if the land tells them what to do: when someone dies, people start cooking. The food initiates and lubricates community. Hot tuna-noodle casseroles and coleslaw in old margarine tubs, steamy fresh rolls and thawing freezer jam must be delivered. When they come to the door with "I'm just dropping this by . . ." it means an hour visit, often with the car motor left running, proving that "I didn't mean to stay long, I know you're awful busy . . ." demonstrating that fellowship with one another has a life of its own, bigger than us, beyond us, which we cannot and do not want to control.

People here talk about death. It is a part of everyday ranch life. Food comes from death. The connection is in your face. Ranch meat comes from an animal that was bred, born, raised, fattened, shot, gutted, hung, skinned, cooled, aged, boned, cut, wrapped and frozen by the eater. Grain is planted, watered, ripened, cut, stored, shipped and bought back as flour, mixed with water and yeast, kneaded and baked. These deaths are essential to life. The logic is intrinsic to the way people make their living: when someone dies people take dead things in their kitchen and form them into gifts that bring life. Life comes from death, and everyone here knows it.

I officiate their funerals, but they heal themselves. They arrive in droves, young and old, to honor their dead and to bless the living. They file past the casket and look inside, not because they've never seen death but because they have and they aren't afraid. They weep without shame, and at the dinner after the service they laugh without restraint.

The ranch environment must be the most materialistic of all worlds. Common sense is not optional, it is law. Life here is not about ideas, it is about what works, what makes things grow, what spells a profit. Montanans know their life comes from the soil, and they revere it.

His Greatest Day

Eighty years of symbiosis with the ground his dad homesteaded schooled the old guy well.

"Soil is the people," the old guy used to tell me.

"Soil is the government," he'd go on.

"Without soil, you have no life; the life is in the soil," he'd argue.

Now he was getting ready to die.

"When I die, my body will go back to the soil; that's what we are, you know, just dirt. And when we die, we turn back into dirt." He didn't seem to mind the thought at all.

But his opinions on fertilization cycles far from exhausted his thoughts on the subject of death.

"When I die, I will see *him*," he said with a defiant confidence. "My soul will go to be with the Lord. He created the whole world, the ground and the streams, the animals, and you and me. And when I die I will go to him. And I will see him face to face. That will be my greatest day."

It was beyond doubt. The deepest and surest thing he'd learned from his long life of living from the soil was the existence of his soul. This lover of the cosmos knew no chasm between spiritual and material realities. He experienced matter and spirit as God's continual life-weaving. He did not recognize a sharp division between life and things.

In the ranch world where life is not a theory but a set of chores, there is an unshakable belief in eternal life. I suppose city folks can wonder if the idea of eternal life derives from the denial of death. Here, where participation in death is a way of life, where mourning is faced with Swedish meatballs, the reality of eternal life is obvious. The spirituality and eternal life of the soul are deep knowledge known softly. It is the still small voice heard beneath the fact that death brings life. It is felt in the soul-chest of a man as the sunset brings pink and orange glowing to the world of chance and toil. As evening falls there is a profound knowing that night is not the end but the beginning.

When the old guy died, it happened just as he said. His body became soil, but he was still alive.

He wasn't tall, but he was very thick. He had the chest, arms and hands of a boxer. His large head did not appear oversized because it perched on a wide neck. The density of his musculature was the kind football players manufacture with steroids. So as he lay dying, when his chest heaved for air the chrome bed frame shook as if a mountain was shifting under his sheets. As a young man out of California, I couldn't help thinking of the movement of tectonic plates.

With every breath his lungs gurgled with water, blood and phlegm. When vermilion and yellow sputum bubbled out of his nose, a family member would gently wipe it away. His chest expanded torturously, unevenly, and every time it collapsed in exhalation it seemed as if this breath must be the last—silence— *will he breathe again?* Our eyes fixed upon his chest. *Will it rise again? Is he gone?* He went on and on, refusing to die. Something inside him would not give up. Body and soul separate under severe protest. Whenever I see this, I stand in pure wonder at the will to live.

The breathing did stop, the heart stopped, his central nervous system died, and then he just wasn't there anymore. Immediately his body began to decay, and his soul went to be with the Lord. Tough as it was, that was one of his greatest days.

The community kicked in. The big funeral dinner needed planning. The grocer volunteered ham, the guy who owned the drive-in brought rolls. Pots went on to boil macaroni. The church ladies fussed over how many to plan for. At the end the family took home several boxes of food to serve the guests who would be stopping by in the coming week.

Eternal Life

It's rather presumptuous to second-guess the old guy about his greatest day, but I think he has a better one coming than the one he fixed his hope on. As great as the day was when his body and soul separated and his soul went to live with Christ, an even better day will be when his body and his soul reunite in the resurrection of the dead and he lives forever in the new heaven and the new earth.

The old guy was notorious for sawing logs through sermons. He was probably snoozin' by the time the subject of the resurrection came up in preaching, or maybe he was thinking about the sow about to give birth, or whether the grain was dry enough to cut, or if that cow moose had bulldozed over the south fence again. Anyway, the old guy has some wonderful surprises ahead in eternal life. And so do we. When in this life we are ambushed by amazement, it is a faint harbinger of the continual incredulity of heaven. We cannot comprehend beforehand the wonder of these events, when our bodies and souls are united forever in a synthesis of being that cannot separate, cannot decay and cannot die.

God is eternal, but he works in and through time. God created the universe in the instant of time when time began. God called our father Abraham on a certain day. He woke up one day an old man, but by the end of that day he was a new man, called to a new land, a new future, a new hope, a new family. Moses was an expatriate herding sheep until one day he saw a burning bush and he approached to see what this thing might mean. That was the last day of his old life. Jesus was born on a day, and he died on a day, and he rose from the grave on a day. The old guy died on a day, and on that day he met Jesus.

The day of the resurrection of the dead will be the greatest day for the old guy, for you and me, and for the whole world of those who believe. In the meantime, until that day, *now* when we die our bodies and souls separate: our bodies return to the dirt (or, I guess, into seawater if we get eaten by a shark), and our souls go to be with the Lord. Theologians give this time of salvation, though it is no *mean* time by any means, a rather inglorious name. They call it the "intermediate state," which sounds like a sentence in the state pen. Or it sounds as if you are waiting in a really, *really* long line to file for an unemployment check.

Jesus calls it "paradise" (Lk 23:43). That is a lot more like what the old guy had in mind. Jesus wants us to think of paradise when we think about what happens to our souls when we die. It is not unreasonable, nor is it unspiritual, to imagine that God has a great day awaiting us when we die, and an even better one further into the future. My guess is that the state we call (unspectacularly) the "intermediate state" may include tours through black holes, fifty-yard-line seats at the birth of new galaxies and face-to-face life with Jesus.

The Scriptures do not tell us a whole lot about life in the intermediate state or about life in the resurrection body. However, we can make some simple biblical observations about what happens when we die and what eternal life is like. This information is critically important for understanding our souls now, in this life.

The Soul Is What Goes to Heaven

The simplest definition of the soul is that the soul is what goes to heaven. That's where we are going to start. In the body, in our life now, the boundaries between body and soul are tough to find. Death, however, and life after death in the intermediate state, gives us a boundary we can really talk about. Putting a telescope on the soul in heaven lets us put a microscope on it here.

Our telescope will be the Bible. The Scriptures of the Old and New Testaments give us roughly the same vantage point on the far reaches of eternal life as a telescope orbiting Earth gives us on the far reaches of the universe.

The naked eye is able to identify stars; we can see more with earthbound telescopes. However, our atmosphere interferes with both ways of seeing. The clearest pictures of distant space come from satellite telescopes circumnavigating Earth beyond the atmosphere. With our spiritual vision humankind in virtually every culture has been able to identify some vague outlines of eternal life, and the highly developed religions can see much more. However, the Bible's vision of eternal life is like the telescope in space: with it we can see beyond the limitations of our human-spiritual atmosphere.

Soul as Essential Self

The testimony of Scripture is clear that when we die our irreducible spiritual self, our soul, enters new life with the Lord. Paul speaks of the departure of his soul at death into the presence of Christ when he muses with the Philippian Christians over what he perceives his dilemma to be: "For to me, living is Christ and dying is gain. If I am to live in the flesh, that means fruitful labor for me; and I do not know which I prefer. I am hard pressed between the two: my desire is to depart and be with Christ, for that is far better" (Phil 1:21-23).

There is no question in Paul's mind that he himself departs when he dies. The self that departs is the soul. Sometimes a speaker in the Scriptures calls the irreducible self that departs "my spirit." The psalmist stated it first with the line "Into your hand I commit my spirit" (Ps 31:5). Jesus immortalized it on the cross: "Then Jesus, crying with a loud voice, said, 'Father, into your hands I commend my spirit.' Having said this, he breathed his last" (Lk 23:46). Stephen followed Jesus' lead but changed the object of his petition: "While they were stoning Stephen, he prayed, 'Lord Jesus, receive my spirit' " (Acts 7:59). In these cases the word *spirit* is a synonym for the word *soul*.[1] Often in the Scriptures *spirit* and *soul* are used synonymously, but not always. In this book we will use the word *soul* to denote the irreducible spiritual self. Later in the book we will look at passages where the word *spirit* denotes something different in us from the word *soul*.

When you die, something that is really you leaves your body and enters life with the Lord. In heaven you are not another person or just any person. Between this life and the next, your soul is your continuous life and identity. Such is the case in this life as well.

Can you ever stop being one person and become another person?

If you lose an arm, do you become another person? If you lose your arms and your legs, do you become another person? If the color of your eyes changed, would you be a different person? If you undergo radical cosmetic surgery, even to the extent of changing your sex, do you become another person? I don't think so.

Soul and Changes in the Brain

How about changes in your brain? A change in the brain is a bodily change that affects consciousness. Does Alzheimer's disease—a disease that destroys brain cells—make you into another person? It may radically alter the shape of your life, your experience of life and the way others experience your life, but does it make you into another person? Alzheimer's destroys memory and diminishes consciousness; both of these functions have traditionally been assigned to the soul. A disease like Alzheimer's presents us with several possibilities for understanding the soul.

One way to look at it is that since Alzheimer's alters consciousness, memory, reasoning, recognition and even spiritual functions, perhaps this proves that functions we have assigned to the soul are nothing but electrochemical reactions in the brain. If this is true, the soul is not spiritual; it is enzymes and electrons that line up and interact to create an illusion of spiritual experience and functions. We must admit this may be true.

On the other hand, if (as I shall attempt to show later) the soul exists and functions in integral union with the body/brain, separable only at death, then as the brain decays or changes it makes sense that the soul's functions would be drastically impaired as well. Granted, this does not prove that the spiritual soul exists. But it does suggest that the curtailing of soul functions when the brain breaks down speaks to us of a spiritual/organic union of brain and soul, the life-weaving work of God, instead of proving that the brain is the whole banana.

In my pastoral work I have learned ways to reach the soul with end-runs around brain damage. You do not need much memory to love being loved, to affirm good or to remember the Word of God.

I visited an elderly gentleman in a nursing home for several years. He was not a member of my congregation, but as I visited members in his room we became friends. One day I approached him with a smile and a handshake and he no longer knew me. He'd had a stroke. I reintroduced myself from scratch, figuring we would just start the friendship over. The damage was more severe than that. He didn't know where he was, he didn't know his own name, he didn't know he was strapped in a wheelchair.

So I just asked him if I could read the Bible to him. I was surprised when, he said, cogently, "Yes, please do."

I began reading Psalm 23, slowly. "The LORD is my shepherd." Pause. His head lifted slightly. He opened his mouth.

"I shall not want," he replied, clearly. I smiled and continued.

"He maketh me to lie down . . ." Pause. I'd seen this kind of thing before.

"In green pastures," came the response.

We continued through the psalm. I prompted him with a line, and he gave me the next one. Near the end, when I said, "Surely goodness and mercy . . ." he rattled off the rest before I could interrupt him: "shall follow me all the days of my life: and I will dwell in the house of the LORD for ever."

When we finished we both smiled and our eyes were not dry. He still didn't know who I was, and he hadn't remembered his name; but in a profound sense he'd refound himself. By using a portion of the Word of God he'd memorized as a child and cherished his whole life, we'd skipped around the damaged cells, and just maybe we found his soul.

The ancient and medieval Catholic divines attributed memory to the soul. That was part of their Platonic inheritance through, among others, Augustine. I'm not sure what to think of that. What I do know is that somehow the Scriptures awakened a portion of my friend's memory invested with spiritual power, which awakened his spiritual consciousness. We stimulated the Word of God stored in his heart from childhood.

Anticipating my argument somewhat later, in Scripture, where *heart* is not a synonym for *soul*—and it often is only that—*heart* is body and soul and spirit become one. *Heart* is where the line between brain and soul is impossible to draw. The Word of God lodged itself in my friend's heart, a place deeper, apparently, than his own name. A place where perhaps the only thing more powerful would have been the sound of his mother's voice. Maybe that's what he heard.

Soul and Identity

Consider persons with severe mental retardation. Some forms of retardation look superficially like Alzheimer's (and stroke damage), but whereas Alzheimer's is a progressive disease, many forms of retardation are stable. Mentally retarded persons stop learning sooner than normal folks, but they usually don't regress. Alzheimer's patients regress. This makes a difference in our perception of the person's spiritual being. Once you get to know a retarded person, there just isn't the same sense of overwhelming sadness and loss as there is with Alzheimer's. This, I think, allows us to view a retarded person as they really are, not from the perspective of what they were or what they might have been. I can speak only for myself, but when I am with retarded persons I have an intense sense of their soul: consciousness, identity, relatedness, will! Even inner vision. Even if their brain is impaired, I don't feel as if their soul is little, or retarded, or even misfunctioning. I sense that the souls of mentally retarded persons are closer to the surface than ours. In this way, retarded persons are often profound spiritual directors.

In everyday life we locate personal identity, in ourselves and in others, in something other than the body and other than consciousness. Consciousness is, after all, a frail thing on which to hang identity. Is a person in a coma or suffering with Alzheimer's another person? Can we change their name? Of course not. Personal identity is more durable than consciousness.

Our personal identity exists as something that changes in the body, including the brain, can affect but not eradicate. Physiological changes of the severest sort cannot eradicate *you*, because even death can't.

Your soul is the real you that survives death. Throughout life it is the you that can be temporarily imprisoned but never erased. In hell, it is the you that is destroyed. Jesus, who cared deeply for the human body, as evidenced by innumerable healings and by his teaching us to pray for our daily bread, warns us against overemphasizing the significance of the body for personal identity and fulfillment. As much as he taught us to care for our bodies, he warns us, "Do not fear those who kill the body but cannot kill the soul; rather fear him who can destroy both soul and body in hell" (Mt 10:28). No matter how serious its condition, a handicapped body is not as serious as a handicapped soul, and a dead body is infinitely less tragic than a dead soul.

Soul Consciousness

Joy. "One of the criminals who were hanged there kept deriding him and saying, 'Are you not the Messiah? Save yourself and us!' But the other rebuked him, saying, 'Do you not fear God, since you are under the same sentence of condemnation? And we indeed have been condemned justly, for we are getting what we deserve for our deeds, but this man has done nothing wrong.' Then he said, 'Jesus, remember me when you come into your kingdom.' He replied, 'Truly I tell you, today you will be with me in Paradise' " (Lk 23:39-43).

This was no time for riddles or parables or symbolic gestures. Jesus answered the penitent thief's petition directly and clearly: the horror they shared that day would soon be replaced by the glorious experience of life in paradise. The thief knew what he meant. *Paradise* was a commonly used word in that day for "the intermediate resting place for the souls of the righteous dead."[2] *Paradise* comes from a Persian word meaning garden or park. In the Judaism of Jesus' day the word referred to the Garden of Eden *and* the bliss of eternal life.[3]

It would be foolish to construct a geography of heaven from such a word, but it would also be a flagrant violation of the plain sense of the text to suggest that the paradise Jesus promised the thief would be a sleepy, semiconscious state. Jesus promises the thief conscious enjoyment in heaven, something like what the old guy figured would be his "greatest day." Better than harping angels cruising around on celestial clouds, the Old Testament prefigures heaven with a metaphor from marriage celebration, a metaphor of joy:

I will greatly rejoice in the LORD,
> my whole being shall exult in my God;
for he has clothed me with the garments of salvation,
> he has covered me with the robe of righteousness,
as a bridegroom decks himself with a garland,
and as a bride adorns herself with her jewels. (Is 61:10)

Joy is the apex of consciousness, and heaven is the apex of joy. The soul is the locus of joy in heaven and on earth.

Even though we experience joy as whole persons, as body and soul indissolubly united in a total experience—after all, what can be more physically joyful than a wedding celebration?—the center of joy is not in the physical sensation of the body but in the spiritual wonder of which the soul is conscious, and which radiates throughout the whole self. The ability to perceive and experience spiritual wonder is a characteristic of the soul. Though the soul is not the whole of consciousness, it is its irreducible element.

Perception. Paul teases us with intimations of an experience he had when he tells us:

> I know a person in Christ who fourteen years ago was caught up to the third heaven—whether in the body or out of the body I do not know; God knows. And I know that such a person—whether in the body or out of the body I do not know; God knows—was caught up into Paradise and heard things that are not to be told, that no mortal is permitted to repeat. (2 Cor 12:2-4)

Paul's immersion in the heavenly milieu is not without parallel in the Scriptures. John tells us of his soul's reception of a heavenly vision as he recalls for us that

> I looked, and there in heaven a door stood open! And the first voice, which I had heard speaking to me like a trumpet, said, "Come up here, and I will show you what must take place after this." At once I was in the spirit, and there in heaven stood a throne, with one seated on the throne! And the one seated there looks like jasper and carnelian, and around the throne is a rainbow that looks like an emerald. Around the throne are twenty-four thrones, and seated on the thrones are twenty-four elders, dressed in white robes, with golden crowns on their heads. Coming from the throne are flashes of lightning, and rumblings and peals of thunder, . . . and in front of the throne there is something like a sea of glass, like crystal. (Rev 4:1-6)

How about the prophet Ezekiel, who received a vision in which "the hand of the LORD came upon me, and he brought me out by the spirit of the LORD and set me down in the middle of a valley; it was full of bones" (Ezek 37:1).

Spiritual seeing, hearing and tasting are not particularly uncommon experiences in the Bible. They are experiences not of semiconsciousness like a dream but of piqued conscious perception, more like mountain climbing than sleepwalking. Here and there, in this life and in the next, the soul is the landing field for divine visions, the screen on which they are projected, a low-frequency receiver picking up discrete supernatural signals.

Furthermore, the soul sees, feels, interprets and comprehends the spiritual meaning in daffodils, holocausts, thrones and dry bones.

Wet to my waist, slogging home down a bone-dry trail, I move quickly, but carefully. I hold my eight-and-a-half-foot-long fly rod out in front of me, low to the ground as I walk, because this is rattlesnake country. I've hiked in and amongst rattlesnakes my whole life and haven't thought much of them, but the Bear Trap Canyon Wilderness of the Madison River is really, really snaky. This trail, used infrequently, exposed to the sun most of the way and full of large, flat granite rocks, is a rattlesnake Riviera.

So far so good. No snakes. I'm feeling pretty good. The trail climbs over a low hump and down into a narrow, six-foot-deep swale, in heavy rocks and brush. Just as I am in the bottom of the swale, when the hump ahead is at eye level, I hear the all-too-familiar shake of the rattle and see a large gray rattler, eight feet from my face, quivering and coiling. It is half-hidden in the dry brush, I cannot see its head, only the gray cylinder moving into strike position amid the gray rocks and the brown grasses. I can't see where it is going or what it is going to do.

I jump back and shudder. I slap the snake with my fly rod, and it scoots away. I climb out of the swale backwards, give a wide berth to the spot on the trail where the snake was, and start hiking again, pretty shook up.

I'd known I would probably see a snake that day. I didn't expect it in my face. No matter where you see it, you can't walk away from being *surprised* by a rattlesnake without an adrenaline rush caused by the instantaneous ignition of the "fight or flight" instinct. And without feeling your soul. The soul perceives not the snake but the death threat, the imminent possibility of the extinguishing of the breath of life. It comprehends the reality of the horror of death, and the gratitude of escape from death, from the perspective of the threat of the loss of personal existence. For as we shall see later, the soul is keenly aware of our very real, very human vulnerability, and the soul is itself very human and very vulnerable. How happy is the soul in the new heaven and the new earth, to be free from the threat of death.

The nursing child shall play over the hole of the asp,
    and the weaned child shall put its hand on the adder's den.
They will not hurt or destroy
    on all my holy mountain;
for the earth will be full of the knowledge of the LORD
    as the waters cover the sea. (Is 11:8-9)

Relationships. "And this is eternal life, that they may know you, the only true God, and Jesus Christ whom you have sent" (Jn 17:3).

Heavenly consciousness of infinite spiritual good, without active relationship with that good, would be hell worse than hell. Rather, heaven is love and knowing.

The Song of Songs in the Old Testament is poetic metaphor both of human love and of divine love. Tension between the two metaphors is built into the song. Is it a story of human love as a metaphor for divine love? Or is it divine love as a metaphor for human love? It is the same dilemma we encounter in a famous Bible verse, 1 John 4:16: "God is love." Does this mean that God is like our (best) human love, or does this mean that God is the definition of love that we must emulate? The double meaning creates a tension in the verse necessary to its practical impact. Likewise, the Song of Songs's double reference creates tension, delivering it from the hands of those who wish to make it into a sex manual or a manual of mysticism. The sacred text possesses power to inflame us with love in every realm.

What *is* certain about the Song of Songs is that many of its passages are the finest examples we have for what heaven will be like relationally, when the dichotomy between sexual union and mystical union will dissolve. It is a body book and it is a soul book. If we try to define the lines, it is our loss.

The Song of Songs teaches us the soul's relational character. Intimate soul relationships are the joy and the goal of our inner life. I have said that joy is the apex of consciousness and that heaven is the apex of joy. The corollary is: knowing Christ is paradise.

Knowing Christ is the paradise of heaven for the thief and for the old guy. When Jesus told the thief, "Truly I tell you, today you will be with me in Paradise," he was telling him something like what Paul told the Corinthian Christians: "For now we see in a mirror, dimly, but then we will see face to face. Now I know only in part; then I will know fully, even as I have been fully known" (1 Cor 13:12). Surely the soul is fitted for and longs for the paradise of knowing and being known in love.

This knowing fully and being fully known is the paradise the soul has lost and has sought ever since the great loss of the paradise of the Garden. The thief and the old guy undoubtedly heard a call to paradise on their great day, and it may well have sounded something like

Arise, my love, my fair one,
    and come away;
for now the winter is past,
    the rain is over and gone.
The flowers appear on the earth;
    the time of singing has come,
and the voice of the turtledove
    is heard in our land.
The fig tree puts forth its figs,
    and the vines are in blossom;
    they give forth fragrance.
Arise, my love, my fair one,
    and come away. (Song 2:10-13)

Two

The Soul
Is Empty

••••••••••••••••••••••••••••••••••••

A synthetic perfume of diesel, bodies, cigarettes, fry oil, coffee and old eggs signifies one thing: a truck stop. The topic of the hastily called meeting was the existence of God.

All I knew when I agreed to the meeting was she *needed to meet with me immediately.* Those were her words. It was Saturday, suppertime, winter, and she was definitely frantic. I figured if she was willing to meet at the truck stop, number one, she must really be desperate; number two, the meeting wouldn't last long; and number three, if she needed to cry, a truck stop is a good place to do that, as any country-music ballad will tell you.

Waiting for our coffee, she thanked me for coming out on such a rotten night. After the waitress sloshed the blackened brew into our cups without a splash, my friend spilled her thoughts in one sentence.

"Nick told me this afternoon he doesn't believe in God anymore."

My first thought was *Why do I need to hear this now, since he would probably still be an atheist on Tuesday?* I couldn't tell if she was afraid for his soul, or for what he might say in church, or if she was just mad at him and wanted to tattle.

"Good," I said definitively. "The God he believed in before wasn't worth believing in anyway; maybe now he can start believing in the real God."[1]

She looked stunned, as you can imagine. Even though I maintained an air of assurance, inside I wondered why I'd said that and how the heck I was going to get out of my verbal predicament. My heart softened. He probably had said that he was an atheist. He had some good reasons for saying it, and she was hurting badly. On the other hand I sensed that my impulsive statement, sponsored by my bad mood, contained possibilities. So I started talking, hoping that something helpful would emerge.

"I guess what I mean is . . . I'm not all that afraid that Nick is really an atheist. I don't think it's going to last that long. And sometimes, ya know, people just have to chuck their old gods before they can really get down to business and get to know God as he really is. I think that's what Nick's doing. Actually I'm kind of hopeful; this could really be a good thing for him."

Her face, which had said *You owe me an apology, Buster!* became thoughtful and introspective. This was *not* one of the options she had considered.

My sympathy for both of them grew as I thought more about their situation. The marriage was in trouble. They were broke. Their kids, two of whom were practically old enough to be her brother and sister, were in trouble with the law.

Nick was a mess. He'd contracted a degenerative neuromuscular disease and couldn't stay employed. She worked two jobs, but they'd lost their home and were forced to move from rental to rental. Of course there were a lot of people around in similar situations: they weren't out of place, not in our town. The thing that always tore my heart out was that they'd run up their credit card on 900-number faith healers.

They'd prayed their way through every setback. Every doctor visit. Every lost job. Every eviction notice. Every trip to the police station to pick up a kid. Nick's confession of betrayal seemed reasonable enough to me.

So I suggested to her, "Nick has rejected God because all along he's thought God is all about success and making it if you live the right way. And now he's discovered that the God he thought he knew doesn't exist."

Her honest fears emerged: "I'm afraid he's going to stop coming to church and that he'll withdraw."

"Yeah, that could happen. In fact it really could happen, and, I guess that is the risk we face."

"But I don't think I should push him."

"You're right. He has to come to God himself. Take the risk. I think he's going to bounce back with a new and real faith."

Amazingly, the thought consoled her. I theologized a little.

"The whole thing revolves around the cross. When Jesus died on the cross he showed us what God is really like and where God really hangs out. God is where pain is. When I go into a room where there is great pain, God is there—before I arrive. I help people recognize that he is already there. The gods of success and prayer technologies can't come to places where people are hurting. They can only condemn people who haven't done it right. I think Nick is just right on the brink of really getting to know God."

This comforted her. She remembered her childhood. She grew up in a drought-plagued, dry-land wheat town, a middle child in a big, broke, Baptist family with a lot of music and church and love. I hadn't affirmed poverty. I'd affirmed emptiness—and she understood that.

This time I guess I hit the mark, because Nick hardly missed a beat in following Christ. He stayed an atheist concerning false gods. His prayer life blossomed.

We don't think of truck stops as monasteries. But a long time ago, monasteries were places where weary travelers could get some modest food, park their load, get some rest and, if they desired, discuss the spiritual concerns of pilgrims.

Space Within: The Form and Material of the Soul

The emptiness within is the vast, vaulted sanctuary where we meet God. Until Christ drives the moneychangers out, as he did out of Nick's soul, none of us can have a peaceful talk with God. Without the soul's emptiness, there is no space for meeting God. This is why the one essential thing we have to say about the architecture of the soul is that it is empty.

Form. In Hans Walter Wolff's masterpiece *Anthropology of the Old Testament,* he entitles his chapter on the Hebrew word for soul, *nephesh,* "Needy Man."[2] Wolff notes that Old Testament writers use the word *nephesh* for "throat," "neck" and "desire."[3] This surprises us: we expect the root meaning of a word like *nephesh* to be something spiritual or something to do with eternal life. Instead the word's usage represents earthiness and vulnerability.

Wolff says about *nephesh,* "When therefore, the throat or neck [is] mentioned, there is frequently an echo of the view of man as needy and in danger, who therefore yearns with his *nephesh* for food and the preservation of his life; and this vital *longing, desiring, striving* or *yearning* can, even when the *nephesh* is mentioned, dominate the concept itself."[4] The Hebrew word for soul is governed by its anatomical, biological root implying neediness, vulnerability and emptiness at the physical and spiritual center of what it means to be human.

This coincides with the Old Testament view of the spiritual nature of the soul. When used in a spiritual sense, *nephesh* connotes longing and weakness, not strength, and certainly not an immortal spirit. That is not to say that the soul cannot live eternally. But all by itself the soul is not an immortal, subsistent spirit. An eternal soul is a saved soul.

Without the Lord the soul is hungry, vulnerable and in constant danger of becoming nothing but a shade. Karl Barth says of the soul's vulnerability,

> And if God were to withdraw what He alone can and does give in this event, not only would his body sink back to the status of a purely material body, to rise and disintegrate even as a material body in the surrounding world of all other bodies, but

he himself would necessarily become a shadow and less than a shadow, a departed soul which once was but now has been, an extinct life.[5]

The soul is empty. It is a bucket, not a geyser. The soul is made to want. This is not due to sin. It is aggravated by sin. Our spiritual vulnerability, our spiritual neediness, our spiritual emptiness is built in—hard-wired, standard circuitry. The essence of sin is the desire to live without God, to be subsistent, to be invulnerable.

A prayer from the Psalms portrays the spiritual reality of the soul's relation to God:

As a deer longs for flowing streams,
   so my soul longs for you, O God.
My soul thirsts for God,
   for the living God.
When shall I come and behold
   the face of God? (Ps 42:1-2)

For Nick, finding God meant becoming empty. For him, and for all of us, without praying, "My God, my God, why have you forsaken me?" (Ps 22:1), we never learn to confess,

Surely goodness and mercy shall follow me
   all the days of my life,
and I shall dwell in the house of the LORD
   my whole life long. (Ps 23:6)

The great Christian mystics, people like St. John of the Cross, Baron von Hügel and Samuel Rutherford, all learned to cherish the emptiness. They knew God precisely at the point of their soul's emptiness and vulnerability. They did not feel independent and self-subsistent. As Rutherford says in a letter to a young student of theology,

I have little of Christ in this prison, but groanings, and longings, and desires. All my stock of Christ is some hunger for Him, and yet I cannot say but I am rich in that. My faith, and hope, and holy practice of new obedience, are scarce worth the speaking of. But blessed be my Lord, who taketh me, light, and clipped, and naughty, and feckless as I am.[6]

He and the other mystics learned these things in times of deprivation and difficulty, just like Nick.

Material. What is the soul made of? The spiritual "material" of the soul is the *event* of the breathing of the soul by the Holy Spirit of God. This breathing makes the soul alive, and thereby makes the body alive, as a material, spiritual whole. In this sense the soul is not spirit; the soul *has* spirit. Karl Barth says it this way: "Man exists because he has spirit. That he has spirit means that he is grounded, and constituted, and maintained by God as the soul of his body."[7] The Bible says it this way: "Then the LORD God formed man from the dust of the ground, and breathed into his nostrils the breath of life; and the man became a living being" (Gen 2:7).

The Holy Spirit continually generates the soul—metaphorically, breathes it. The "Breath of Life" is not exactly the Holy Spirit. It is the *event* of the Holy Spirit generating human life.

So what kind of stuff is the soul made of? We might call it *event-stuff.* The soul isn't really describable by a noun or a verb. It is like a noun because it really is something. But it is like a verb because it exists only insofar as it is an action. The human soul is the irreducible human-spiritual self generated by the event of the breath of life, and it is itself an event, an occurrence. It is a thing in that it happens; when it no longer happens, it ceases to exist.

The "thing" that the Holy Spirit generates is a fully human spiritual existence. The soul is not a divine thing, or a divine spark. It is a fully human, spiritual existence. It exists in spiritual analogy to the Holy Spirit of God. The soul is not a spiritual offspring of the Holy Spirit. It is a living human-spiritual image of the Holy Spirit in life, through death into eternal life, but not in eternal death. When the soul leaves the body at death, the Holy Spirit continues its generation in eternal life. Not so in hell. In hell the Holy Spirit no longer generates the soul. That *is* hell.

It's hard to say what the soul is like in hell. It isn't all gone, nor is it all there. What remains is a shadow of the former self, something two-dimensional like a cartoon: a spiritual tombstone, a name plate with memories.

The Soul Filled: The Sea Sponge

The soul is like a sea sponge. The sponge is a simple sea creature whose form, material and function are rather like a lung without a body. The sponge fills itself with what it is in—seawater. Using flagella to move the water in and through and out of its body, the sponge draws seawater in, harvests oxygen and nutrients, metabolizes them and exhales carbon dioxide and other nutrients. That is its whole life. The soul works like that.

Like the sponge, the soul is filled with what it is *in*. This sounds hard to understand, but it really isn't. It's what we mean when we say, "I am in love."

When we are *in love,* our soul is filled with love. It is filled with love because we are in a relationship of love. The love is in us, but the love comes from the relationship of love that we are in. The relationship of love is not in us. What a horribly self-centered view of love that would be! Love relationships fill our souls with love.

The same kind of thing happens in our relationship with Christ. As we are *in* Christ, we are *filled* with the Holy Spirit.

The late C. F. D. Moule, professor at Cambridge University, observes in his little book *The Phenomenon of the New Testament,* "Christians are thought of . . . as having their very location, existence and status in Christ; whereas Christ is *not*—or only seldom—spoken of correlatively as thus existing in Christians."[8] He goes on to note, however, that the Christian's relationship with the Holy Spirit is nuanced differently. "It is a striking observation . . . that broadly speaking, the reverse holds true for the Pauline phrases with the Spirit: the idea of the Spirit as being in Christians is more a fundamental idea than that of Christians as being in the Spirit."[9]

This is not theological jibberjabber. It has spiritual, practical importance for understanding Christian spirituality and the soul. To be *filled* with the Spirit, you must be *in* Christ. To be in Christ means to live in the kingdom of God and to be in the body of Christ, the church. There is simply no Christian spiritual inner life without the Christian outer life of being in fellowship with other believers.

The apostle John says much the same thing in his admonition to a church about to dissolve: "Those who say, 'I love God,' and hate their brothers and sisters, are liars; for those who do not love a brother or sister whom they have seen, cannot love God whom they have not seen" (1 Jn 4:20). The life of the soul in the Spirit of Christ is established in love that is physical. It is a communion of whole persons, body and soul, for whom, as for the old guy, there is no chasm between spiritual and material realities. As James puts it, "Religion that is pure and undefiled before God, the Father, is this: to care for orphans and widows in their distress, and to keep oneself unstained by the world" (Jas 1:27).

What Is the Human Spirit?

The sea sponge cannot survive in tap water. The seawater in which the sponge lives and metabolizes is a bafflingly complex mixture of water, salt and millions of microscopic organisms, organic compounds and elements—the chicken soup of life. The spiritual environment the soul lives in and "metabolizes" is also bafflingly complex. The water environment of the sea sponge has many ingredients but one name, seawater. The spiritual environment of the soul has many ingredients but one name, spirit.

"Spirit" in this sense of the word is a bafflingly complex mixture of many spiritual realities. I say "spiritual realities" because to say that we are filled with spirits makes it sound as if we are filled with demons. Some people are filled with demons, but that is not what I mean here. Our human spirit is that complex of emotions, values, spiritual gifts and spiritual power that indwell us and define us to ourselves and those around us.

A good example is found in Paul's first letter to the Corinthians: "For though absent in body, I am present in spirit; and as if present I have already pronounced judgment in the name of the Lord Jesus on the man who has done such a thing. When you are assembled, and my spirit is present with the power of our Lord Jesus . . ." (1 Cor 5:3-4). Paul is discussing how to handle a touchy situation of church discipline. He is not able to be physically present to help the church in this difficult matter. By saying that he would be present in spirit, Paul did not mean that his soul would leave his body and show up at the Corinthians' church meeting! Instead he meant that his ideas, values and commands, and the spiritual power represented by his apostleship and his prayers, would be present as the church met. In this sense the presence of his spirit meant Paul's personal power as a Christian, a missionary and an apostle. Thus Paul's spirit is something that he is filled with, that his soul is filled with. Although it represents his thoughts, feelings, gifts and calling, it does not represent his personal, spiritual self, generated by the Holy Spirit. In this sense Paul's spirit differs from his soul.

What are we made of: two things, body and soul, or three things, body, soul and spirit? It may appear that I am saying we are made of three things—body, soul and spirit. However, as the argument unfolds it will become apparent that I believe we are made of two things, body and soul.

Spirit is a cipher for our spiritual attributes, like being courageous or timid. To say that our eyes are blue is not to say that we have eyes and we have blue. Likewise, our souls are characterized by their spiritual qualities.

This requires more explanation. We need to look at what Scripture says about the various terms it uses to describe us. What makes this so complicated is that, as I said earlier, often the words *spirit* and *soul* are synonyms. In Acts 7:59, "While they were stoning Stephen, he prayed, 'Lord Jesus, receive my spirit,' " *spirit* is a synonym for *soul.* Yet such is not always the case. What do all these terms mean? The church has riddled over this issue for centuries, but there is a general consensus.

The Scriptures of the Old and New Testaments use three main words to denote and describe our spiritual nature. They are *soul, spirit* and *heart* (heart will be discussed in detail in the third chapter). The church has wondered for two millennia whether the soul and the spirit are two different parts of our spiritual nature or whether these words are synonyms for one, indivisible spiritual nature.

The view that body, soul and spirit are different parts of human nature is called "trichotomy." The view that we exist in two parts, body and soul/spirit—these two being considered synonyms—is "dichotomy," or "dualism." The view that we are whole beings without distinctions between body, soul and spirit is "monism."

In the first chapter I disavowed monism. What about the soul and spirit? Are they two different things? John W. Cooper, in *Body, Soul and Life Everlasting*, provides an excellent discussion of these distinctions, and I will take the liberty to quote him at length. Speaking of the early Christian thinkers, he tells us:

> Some held that humans consist of three parts—body, soul and spirit. They are called "Trichotomists," since they divide human nature into three components. Spirit is the essential human self which relates to God. Soul is that dimension of persons which mediates and conjoins the spirit with the material body. The trichotomistic view was more popular among the Greek and Alexandrian church fathers who were influenced by Plato, among them Clement of Alexandria, Origen, and Gregory of Nyssa.
>
> It is the other option, "dichotomy," which emerged as the more dominant and eventually orthodox view. It was popular from the beginning among the Latin fathers and given lasting status by Augustine. It is the view that humans consist of two dimensions or components, body and soul/spirit. Dichotomists generally take "soul" and "spirit" as synonyms. Death cuts the body and soul apart. Hence the term "dichotomy."[10]

The Protestant Reformers did not veer from Catholic orthodoxy on this issue. Calvin, for instance, was a dualist. In the twentieth century Karl Barth rejected trichotism with the pungent observation "Trichotism must necessarily issue in the view and concept of two different souls and therefore in a splitting of man's being. This makes understandable the force with which it was condemned at the Fourth Council of Constantinople in A.D. 867-70."[11] So much for trichotism.

Nevertheless, the anthropological terms for the spiritual nature, *spirit* and *heart*, will not go away. *Heart* is the most important term in both Testaments for referring to the inner nature. Why aren't we "quadrachotomists"? Another important term for the inner nature is *bowels*. Why aren't we considering becoming "pentachotomists"? Paul distinguishes between *body* and *flesh*. That would make us "sextachotomists." That one just might catch on.

We have entered the wilderness of biblical word study. Our best guide, the Sacajawea of lexicographers, is Hans Walter Wolff. He steers us clear of the quicksand of thinking that each specific word denotes a different and specific part of the human being. "Concepts like heart, soul, flesh and spirit (but also ear and mouth, hand and arm) are not infrequently interchangeable in Hebrew poetry."[12] A good example would be

The LORD is near to the broken*hearted*,
   and saves the crushed in *spirit.* (Ps 34:18)

Wolff recommends what he calls "stereometric thinking."[13] This is a cool phrase until you try to figure out exactly what it means. In my mind it conjures up a sound system blasting out rock 'n' roll (this is not what our distinguished German professor had in mind). But anyway, music playing in different tracks of a stereo system simultaneously fuses in our minds into a pleasing experience evocative of a live performance. Likewise, Scripture presents us with different metaphors of what it means to be human. As they meet us, they fuse into a pleasing and realistic picture. For instance, when Jesus tells us, "You shall love the Lord your God with all your heart, and with all your soul, and with all your mind" (Mt 22:37), if we just listen to it we understand it: we are to love God with every fiber of our being. If we try to figure out what it means to love God with all our heart, and then with all our soul, and then with all our mind, we get all gooped up in the anthropology and lose the point.

This is the truth inherent in monism—the view that we are not body and soul, or body and soul and spirit, but inseparable, whole beings. The essential teaching of the Old and New Testaments is that we are whole beings—that's what the old guy believed. But that doesn't mean the old guy was a monist. The different terms used in the Bible for human nature connote different aspects of our being.

What then is the difference between soul and spirit? It is vital to remind ourselves that in Scripture, most of the time, *there is no difference at all;* they are synonyms, period. Such is the case in the following verse:

Therefore I will not restrain my mouth;
I will speak in the anguish of my *spirit;*
I will complain in the bitterness of my *soul.* (Job 7:11)

However, in some passages *spirit* means something very different from *soul.*

But my servant Caleb, because he has a different *spirit* and has followed me wholeheartedly, I will bring into the land into which he went, and his descendants shall possess it. (Num 14:24)

When the company of prophets who were at Jericho saw him at a distance, they declared, "The *spirit* of Elijah rests on Elisha." (2 Kings 2:15)

The LORD has poured into them
a *spirit* of confusion;
and they have made Egypt stagger in all its doings
as a drunkard staggers around in vomit. (Is 19:14)

Because an excellent *spirit,* knowledge, and understanding to interpret dreams, explain riddles, and solve problems were found in this Daniel . . . (Dan 5:12)

For though absent in body, I am present in *spirit.* (1 Cor 5:3)

When *spirit* is not a synonym for *soul,* it usually means that which differentiates us from others. In these passages and others like them, *spirit* implies particular emotions, charismatic gifts, intellectual qualities, in groups and in individuals.

No definite rules exist to help us decide when *spirit* is a synonym for *soul* and when it means something different. Common sense may be our best tool here, as it is for much biblical interpretation.

Cataloging the human spirit would be an enormous task. It would involve distinguishing the spiritual qualities of nations, cultures and languages, and the roles and values of the sexes, age groups and social standings within those groups. And of course each individual within each group has a different spiritual makeup as well.

We can describe the human soul, but we must catalog the human spirit. The difference is like hearing an allergist describe the human immune system, which is essentially one thing, and then catalog the unbelievable numbers of possible allergies. The structure and functions of our souls are basically the same, but our spirits are very different. The differences between our spirits is determined to a large degree by the body and the family and culture that each of our souls is *in.*

The male human soul and female human soul are the same. But there is a difference between the spirit of being male and the spirit of being female. How does this work? The insight that the soul is filled by what surrounds it assists our understanding.

The Soul-Sponge Filled

The soul is in the body as a sea sponge is in the sea. The body surrounds the soul, saturates it, and so the soul "breathes" the body's characteristics. The body fills the soul with feelings, thinking and drives.

A female body fills the soul with the spiritual qualities inherent in being female. That is far from saying that the quality of being female is one thing. Females differ spiritually in as many possible ways as there are different physical manifestations of being female. Furthermore, a human soul in a female body is in more than a female body; it is also in a community of human beings who value females differently. The same holds true for males.

Each particular female and male, as different as they may be, is differentiated further by an unpredictable variable, the will.

The will is, I believe, located in the soul. The will is, among other things, each person's ability to choose the spiritual environment his or her soul breathes.

Can the will of the soul and the spirit of the body be in conflict? Absolutely. Experts on alcoholism will often wax on about alcoholism as a physical disease, shortly thereafter address it as a spiritual problem, and end their discourse with a statement that alcoholics are not bad people. I believe each of these theses. However, it is far from clear exactly how they fit together.

If what I am saying here about body, soul and spirit is true, those three ideas about alcoholism are not inconsistent. Our understanding of body, soul and spirit help us to see how they are true and illustrates the conflict in the life of an alcoholic. We know that some people are more physically susceptible to alcoholism than others. That appears now to be a medical fact. (I suspect that eventually what we now call the "addictive personality" will also prove to have a physiological root.) If this is true, then people with that body makeup also have the spiritual qualities that lead to alcoholism in their soul. Compound this with the fact that people who grow up in alcoholic families "inherit" these psychological characteristics through nurture, and you begin to get the idea that alcoholism really is a spiritual disease. This, however, does not make the alcoholic's soul bad. Alcoholism does not make someone into a bad person. And so, usually, the alcoholic's soul is in dread conflict with an alcoholic's spirit. The soul is willing, but the spirit is stronger, until the spirit threatens to overrun the soul entirely. But the soul can be awakened and made stronger through the miracle of love, and the spirit can be harnessed and disciplined through the miracle of confrontation.

When things go right, recovering alcoholics are extremely careful about the environment they allow their soul to be in. Choices to walk into a bar, into an AA meeting, into a church or into the house of a friend who drinks are all deeply spiritual decisions for alcoholics. It matters acutely to them what physical environment their soul is in—because every physical environment is also a spiritual environment, as the old guy would be happy to tell you.

Am I touting a form of trichotism? No, because a person without spirit can be very much alive. Alzheimer's disease curtails the soul's spiritual functions by damaging the body, but the soul is not damaged. As the disease progresses, the brain damage alters spirituality until it is virtually eliminated. It would not be unusual to say of an Alzheimer's patient, "He has no more spirit." It would be unconscionable to say, "He no longer has a soul." Though the patient's spirit is virtually nonexistent, the body and the soul are present and alive. The Holy Spirit breathes the soul as ever, without diminution.

When we go to heaven, we do not take our broken human spirit with us. Our essential self goes to heaven, but much is left behind. And thank goodness. Who wants to take the spiritual characteristics of addiction to heaven? Who wants to take the spirituality of depression to heaven? Who wants to take lust to heaven? And Jesus tells us that being male and female is not a big deal in heaven—if it is anything at all.

That is not to say there is no spirit in heaven! But the joy is being filled with a new and right spirituality. What a wonder it will be for David's prayer to be answered in fullness: "Create in me a clean heart, O God, and put a new and right spirit within me" (Ps 51:10).

Three

Fuel,
Air & Spark

······································

*I*n *Anthropology of the Old Testament* Hans Walter Wolff entitles his chapter on the heart "Reasonable Man." Wolff calls the Hebrew word for heart *(leb* or *lebab)* "the most important word in the vocabulary of the Old Testament anthropology."[1] Taken together, these Hebrew words occur 858 times in the Old Testament, making them "the commonest of all anthropological terms."[2] In the Old Testament heart is the locus for feelings, desires, reason and above all the will.[3]

Heart and Soul

Several crucial Scriptures use *heart* and *soul* synonymously. The point in each case is that acting with *heart* and with *soul* means acting with the whole self.

We love the Lord with all our heart and soul: "Hear, O Israel: The LORD is our God, the LORD alone. You shall love the LORD your God with all your heart, and with all·your soul, and with all your might" (Deut 6:4-5).

We seek the Lord with all our heart and soul: "From there you will seek the LORD your God, and you will find him if you search after him with all your heart and soul" (Deut 4:29).

We serve the Lord with all our heart and soul: "Take good care to observe the commandment and instruction that Moses the servant of the LORD commanded you, to love the LORD your God, to walk in all his ways, to keep his commandments, and to hold fast to him, and to serve him with all your heart and with all your soul" (Josh 22:5).

We make covenant with God with all our heart and our soul: "They entered into a covenant to seek the LORD, the God of their ancestors, with all their heart and with all their soul" (2 Chron 15:12).

We store up the Word of God in our heart and our soul: "You shall put these words of mine in your heart and soul, and you shall bind them as a sign on your hand, and fix them as an emblem on your forehead" (Deut 11:18).

To repent we must return to God with our heart and soul: "if they repent with all their heart and soul in the land of their captivity, to which they were taken captive, and pray toward their land, which you gave to their ancestors" (2 Chron 6:38).

Christian unity is a matter of heart and soul: "Now the whole group of those who believed were of one heart and soul, and no one claimed private ownership of any possessions, but everything they owned was held in common" (Acts 4:32).

Genuine love, from the heart, comes from a purified soul: "Now that you have purified your souls by your obedience to the truth so that you have genuine mutual love, love one another deeply from the heart" (1 Pet 1:22).

The Word of God divides the undividable—heart, soul, spirit, thoughts and intentions: "Indeed, the word of God is living and active, sharper than any two-edged sword, piercing until it divides soul from spirit, joints from marrow; it is able to judge the thoughts and intentions of the heart" (Heb 4:12).

Heart and *soul* are synonymous, with this qualification: *heart* designates soul from the perspective of the integration of body and soul. Heart *expresses* what it means to be whole, thinking, feeling, creative and even depressed people. The soul is our irreducible spiritual center. The heart is our spiritual center from the perspective of the soul's utter integration with all that it means to be human.

When I think of the heart, I think of Vera.

An Afternoon with Vera

Vera's double knits hung loosely on her slender frame. Her arms dangled from her shoulders like bent nails. She couldn't walk too far, so when we toured the nursing home visiting the old people, I pushed her in a wheelchair. Vera was eighty, and she wasn't too proud to be in a wheelchair; actually she was too proud to care about it. To her vanity was so much foolishness.

She frequently recommended that I try vinegar on pancakes. For some reason it tasted sweet to her.

One day I asked her if she was a Calvinist. She got this quizzical look on her face, as if I'd asked a Presbyterian spinster a really dumb question. "Of course I am. Aren't you? How can you not be?"

"How can you not be?" I repeated to myself softly, under my breath, smiling, shaking my head. She gave good answers. I didn't think she'd heard me.

"Well, how *can* you not be a Calvinist?" she insisted. (She *had* heard me.) "Doesn't it say that all good gifts come from God?"

I didn't argue; her Scottish logic was tough.

Every Tuesday we visited old folks. Some were old friends of hers, some were church members, some were friends we made along the way. It didn't matter to Vera. She treated them all the same: with respect. What a conversationalist she was! She listened carefully to every word, synthesizing what she heard with what she saw—she read facial nuances brilliantly—to gain a clear and utterly sympathetic understanding. Furthermore, she knew when old people had finished what they had to say. She didn't let them get caught in that uncomfortable conversation-loop where you keep talking, repeating yourself, because you can't end a thought.

When her turn came she spoke her mind. She enunciated her words flawlessly, speaking slowly enough to be understood, but quickly enough so she never talked down. When the time came for tenderness, she was never short of that.

Words came easily to her and always had. She'd been an English teacher. She enjoyed lecturing me about the vital importance of diagramming sentences for those learning the English language. Once I mentioned to her that diagramming sentences was impossible for me in school.

"Fiddlesticks," she said. "You had a bad teacher."

Neither of us doubted that she could have taught me how to diagram sentences. She had a snappy way of answering questions that lent dignity to both her listener and herself. You always came away from her feeling smarter.

One day after our rounds, as we stood outside her nursing home soaking up some winter sun, she shocked me by saying out of the blue: "I had a man friend once."

I stood silently, waiting for her next sentence.

"We were young, and he was beautiful—just *beautiful.*" She paused.

Tilting her head up and cocking it just slightly, she peered into the sky, looking to the place that stored her memories. That was how she always remembered things. She didn't go inside to remember; she always looked up, as if her memories were recorded in another world. I swear it seemed as if she were reading her life off God's Book.

"He was strong, and oh, was he good-looking . . ." She gasped and paused. The picture startled her; her heart caught its beat. "I loved him with all my heart.

"He kissed me once," she said. Now her eyes closed and she bowed her head. Her deep and honest modesty applied restraint, but she didn't give in. The reticence was part of the drama.

"When he kissed me—oh!" Again she gasped and paused.

"I will never forget it. Electricity passed through me, from his lips to mine, back and forth through my body."

She became realistic and looked me in the eyes.

"We broke up. I went my way, he went his, and we never saw each other again, and that was that." She stopped, then continued.

"Heaven will be like that kiss," she mused.

For a minute she stood as if she were alone; her thoughts followed a rabbit trail in her memory. She revealed nothing of what she saw. And I most certainly did not ask.

The Soul at Work

We experience ecstasy and anguish as whole persons, body and soul. But that tells us little. It's like saying we don't drive an engine or a chassis but a whole car. So what? How much help is that when your car is broken down?

You limp your Volvo into a Montana town with a main street as long as a wink. A sign provides some relief: "Foreign Car Specialist."

You feel darned lucky. The mechanic is in.

"My car isn't working. It sputters and pops and it's smoking. Can you fix it for me? I'm late for an appointment in One Horse."

The mechanic looks at your out-of-state plates and toys in his mind with what business you—or anyone for that matter—might have in One Horse. He cynically surmises a land deal or a visit from the IRS.

So the lotus flower grease monkey retorts: "Your car is a whole entity. I can't work on it as if it had *parts*. That kind of thinking does violence to the integrity of the whole car. My real concern is for the *whole car* . . ." He's just warming up.

You turn your head in disgust and notice behind his shop ten rotting Volkswagens. Shoot straight with him.

"Listen, Aristotle! Fix the car so I can get going!"

With an off-kilter grin, having enjoyed tweaking your nose, he will fix every problem your car has, including some it doesn't.

Even things that work as wholes have parts.

When an engine doesn't work, the mechanic checks out the three essentials of combustion: fuel, air and spark. Our heart, the inner, spiritual self, functions similarly. The heart is the human combustion chamber where fuel, air and spark meet, ignite and explode, where the energy is channeled and we are moved.

Here's how Vera's worked.

The *fuel* came from her body. Her brain stored the memory of the kiss. In recalling that memory her body felt the kiss again. It was definitely a physical experience for her. She felt it again, through her whole body. To be honest, I recall turning a bit red just listening to her.

The *air* came from her spirit. She was a plucky, modest, honest woman who had lived her life by steel virtues and a genuine love for all that is truly human and good. She cherished the kiss. She had come to terms with the fact that the relationship did not work out. It was in a sense vinegar, but somehow it tasted sweet to her. She was after all a Calvinist, the best, gentlest type. Nothing in her life came by accident. She used the word *luck* only begrudgingly, in crossword puzzles.

Vera's *spark* came from the breath of life. She was alive. Her twisted spine, susceptible lungs and overworked, underfueled physical heart never diminished the greater fact that she had life, she loved life, and the life in her generated energy.

Previously I said that the soul is empty like a sea sponge. In one sense it is empty, but in another sense it is full. The sea sponge metabolizes the nutrients in seawater. Similarly, the soul metabolizes the spiritual resources in its environment.

Metabolism is a good metaphor for how the soul functions, but it does not capture the vitality of a soul like Vera's. Great athletes are metabolic marvels. But the fastest sprinters in the world can't keep up with the gross speed and raw power of Vera's soul. Hers was an internal combustion engine. Whereas Vera's blood pump was always on the brink of breaking down, her heart was a twenty-four-valve screamer.

Filled with explosive stuff and lit, the human soul bursts with thought, desire, faith, denial, will, anguish and courage. The heart is the spiritual combustion chamber of human existence.

Sometimes the human combustion chamber sputters and pops and loses power. Sometimes it just won't start. This is depression, the disease of the human heart.

Depression

Depression's symptoms concern the heart: a lack of energy, a sometimes subtle and sometimes profound failure of the will to live, unclear thinking, loss of nerve, anxiety, a sense of fear and paranoia, the evaporation of hope. Depression is a "heart" disease in that it is a sickness in the center of what it means to be human. Its genesis can be physical, emotional or spiritual, or any combination of the three. It takes a metaphor as complex as "heart" to describe the origins of depression.

If we think of the heart as the human combustion chamber, depression is a failure of the human engine. When an internal combustion engine fails or falters, the problem is usually with fuel, air or spark. It may be helpful to see the problem of depression in the same way.

Sometimes depression is a fuel problem. The heart's fuel comes from the body. Depression is frequently a physical problem. Brain chemistry disorders, nutritional problems and other sicknesses can all cause depression. For this type of depression one is advised to see a physician.

Sometimes depression is an air problem. This is what we might call the psychological source of depression. The heart's air is the human spirit. The human spirit is the vast resource of humanness in which the soul dwells. The human spirit is affected by many things in us and around us—like the flu or the morning paper or spring's violet crocus pushing its way through a crust of snow. Human loss, bad relationships and guilt can cause depression. We repress anger, and anger causes depression. We repress bad memories, and bad memories can cause depression. We repress fear, and fear causes depression. We repress guilt, and guilt causes depression. Sometimes identifying the unconscious sources of depression releases some of its control over us. Often this kind of depression takes much longer to deal with and requires arduous psychotherapy.

Sometimes depression is a spark problem. The Holy Spirit generates the heart's spark in its continual breathing of the soul. Spark is the will to live. In an even deeper sense the spark is life.

It isn't exactly the soul, and it isn't exactly the Holy Spirit. Spark is the rhythm, the oscillation, the energy emanating from the generation of the soul. When the fuel and the air are present in the heart in balanced mixture, the spark lights it off. When spark is the problem, the depression is spiritual in genesis.

When spark is the problem, the spark's intensity or timing is usually off-kilter. The spark may be too weak to light the fuel and the air. When the spark comes at the wrong time during the compression cycle—too late or too early—the problem is timing; in that case the fuel and air burn incompletely or not at all.

The Spirit's breathing may generate various intensities of spark and different timing. Sometimes the Holy Spirit lessens the intensity of the spark, or changes the timing, to teach us something new, to alter our course in life or to force us to seek God more fervently.

Floyd: Cooling Spark

Following a period of appreciably decreased activity in our fellowship, Floyd tried some other churches. His defection did not last long. Changing seats didn't help. His spiritual apathy continued, and he felt helpless to do anything about it. It impinged on his whole life.

Floyd was depressed. He didn't know what the problem was. He'd tried different theories. For a while the church was at fault: the rest of us weren't as committed as before. For a while it was my fault: I needed to be more active in leadership. Now he was taking the blame himself. There were some old sins from a long time ago he was still ashamed of. He also thought God was punishing him for letting his morning devotions go by the wayside.

Floyd couldn't get past a golden era in his spiritual life. He had served on numerous committees, attended every service and taught Sunday school. Whew! Just listening to the schedule he admired exhausted me. I became convinced that Floyd's depression was a message from God. God had cooled Floyd's spark so he would slow down.

Floyd needed quiet. He needed to listen God, his family and

his own heart. He definitely needed to go fishing. I prescribed long walks. "Take your wife out on a date," I suggested.

Floyd's hyperactive religiosity came from his need to earn something from God and impress us. God didn't need anything from Floyd. We didn't either. God communicated a positive message to Floyd hidden in the depression: "I love you even when you aren't busy."

Ruby: Out of Sync

Ruby hadn't seemed herself, so I asked how she was doing.

"Oh, not that great. I'm tired. I'm thinking about resigning from council. My whole life is in an uproar; it all seems pointless."

She was down. Underneath her pleasant smile she harbored resentment, doubts and resignation. Her faith wasn't helping her out of her fix.

"I just feel like my life is constantly in chaos," she said.

That was hardly what outsiders thought about her. Ruby's ducks were all in a row. Her work, her family, her faith, her exercise and her reading all fit neatly into an ordered existence. Her needs and goals were being met, and she was helping a lot of other people. Ruby was not self-centered. She only appeared self-centered to people who lacked her discipline and drive. Ruby was envied. She both despised it and craved it.

Ruby was a garden-variety sinner. She didn't mind repentance. She was good at it. She'd self-diagnosed some control issues from her past, and she'd seen a doctor. Nothing seemed to make a difference.

My conclusion was that the disorder in her life came from God. He was throwing her timing off. God never let her get settled. He wasn't angry with her; she wasn't being disciplined for sin; she just needed to let go. Ruby's life wasn't out of control, and it certainly wasn't failing in any sense except one: she wasn't enjoying it. God was making her life not work to make her angry, frustrated and depressed, and unable to fix it with any system or discipline she could devise.

Ruby was attempting to override God's timing in her life by

her own will. As she learned to let her life (and the lives of those around her) just occur a little more, she rediscovered laughter and conversational prayer. As her ducks left their row and began to swim freely in the pond of her mind, the ripples and loose feathers on the water made her reflection go away. She rose and moved about life freely. Her prayer list, the longest and best kept in the church, got lost and she never replaced it.

Unconscious Harbor

Karl Barth remarks,

> How much harm comes from the forcible suppression of memories contrary to the will of God: memories which we ought to have, but for some reason or other seek to avoid; memories which we try to conceal under images of the present and the future, but which God Himself has not concealed; memories which we cannot really succeed in obliterating, but which merely become the cause of psychological disorders. Enforced oblivion is as bad as enforced recollection.[4]

Where does repressed anger reside in us? From whence do fears apply their relentless pressure on our lives? What in us does the work of repression? The answer is the unconscious.

I see the awesome reality of the unconscious and its powerful force every day in pastoral work. I see it in the lives of the people I work with and in my own life. It is no exaggeration to call our conscious life a mere tip of the colossal iceberg of our whole mind. The bulk of our mental work takes place beneath the water line of consciousness. Any pastor who does not take the unconscious processes into account will repeatedly run aground on them. I discuss one of the unconscious processes pastors must deal with, transference and countertransference, in my book *The Art of Pastoring*.

It is of no little consequence that in some traditions pastors are called "father." We are authority figures with love, so like it or not, we symbolize parents to people. For adults who have had positive relationships with their parents, this creates little problem. They have respect and love for their parents. Likewise, they have a natural respect and love for pastors.

But in cases where the relationship with the parent was deeply faulted, people develop something like an ideal parental construct and transfer this to anyone like a parent—and especially someone who gives them love as a parent should have in the first place. Parishioners can superimpose this ideal parental figure over the pastor; they "fall in love"—not with the pastor, but with the pastor as the incarnation of their ideal parental figure. Then they shift the monumentally important childhood desire to please their parent, which was never satisfied by their natural parents, onto the pastor.[5]

The results of this attachment can appear to be advantageous. The parishioner may undergo a "transference cure."[6] This happens when a person complies with an authority figure in order to please him or her—for example, someone trying to please a pastor may become a Christian. The person experiences a genuine sense of relief. After all, they have finally pleased their "parent." But these "conversions" don't last very long. A parishioner experiencing transference can "love" a pastor deeply, as their ideal parent, for a while; then, without warning, their emotions shift and they displace intense anger toward their parent onto the pastor. One minute they are worshiping their ideal parent, the next they are punishing their real parent—all in the person of the pastor.

I wonder sometimes whether the displacement of anger following love isn't inevitable. Sometimes it seems as if the displacement of anger to a substitute parent was the unconsciously preconceived design of the drama from the start. Meanwhile the pastor, eager to please, enters the fog of countertransference, in which feelings of love for his or her own parent are transferred to the parishioner.

Perhaps this arrangement sounds dangerous to you. It is. Especially if sexual passion gets mixed in. Certainly many clergy extramarital disasters are transference/countertransference affairs. Whatever else might cause them, these debacles are never expressions of conscious, mature sexual behavior.

This does not begin to describe the hellish existence many pastors' wives[7] live through as they become the objects of displaced anger at Mother or Sister. The silent but steady rage they endure often exceeds the attacks their husbands endure.

On the other hand, explosions of human creativity are unthinkable apart from the unconscious. Poetry is our unconscious connections of pictures, words, sounds and meanings leaking out to consciousness line by line. Even the grueling process of revision, the overtly conscious effort to make the poem better, may simply be an attempt to orient the material more accurately to the voice one hears faintly within. This may explain why a piece of poetry or prose requires many drafts before it sounds like the author's voice.

Maybe creative people—artists, writers, inventors and the like—have more permeable barriers between their conscious and unconscious minds. That may explain their propensity for depression and other forms of mental illness.

The Unconscious and the Soul
But what does this all have to do with the soul? Is the unconscious mind the soul?

Our direct experience of our soul is tiny compared to the vast workings of our soul, most of which we do not feel. Perhaps the ratio of conscious thought to unconscious thought holds true for our experience of the soul. Perhaps this is why the soul and the unconscious are difficult to describe and to understand. Does that mean they are the same thing? No.

The unconscious is the inaccessible aspect of what I have been calling the heart. It certainly involves the soul. The unconscious deserves the term *self.* But there is so much in the unconscious that is separable from the true self. There is much in the unconscious that the true self is better off without.

Freud was right. The unconscious is a reservoir of drives, fears and desires. The unconscious assigns symbolic objects to unthinkable thoughts. The pressure created by unconscious displacement really does drive us nuts. Jesus spoke truly when he said, "And you will know the truth, and the truth will make you free" (Jn 8:32). The "you" that truth sets free is the real you. The fears, the doubts and the violence within aren't the real you. Healing, whatever the method, is the process of separating your true self from the falsehood you have misidentified as your true self.

This isn't the problem of sin.[8] Recalling the argument of the second chapter that the soul is filled with spirit and that the spirit which fills us is a complex mix of many spiritual realities, what I mean here is that a process exists for separating our soul from its self-identification with false spiritual realities.

At issue here is whether a mentally ill person is a whole human being. Must we treat mentally ill people as whole human beings made in the image of God? Of course we must. Because we feel sorry for them? Or because they are in full possession of that which makes them fully human? They fully possess that which makes them human: they are souls made in the image of God. Their souls are impaired by a body and an unconscious that don't work correctly. We cannot deny them the rights of human beings—civil, spiritual and personal.

The Soul and Evil Spirits

I have spoken about spiritual realities filling the soul. What about spirit beings filling the soul—how about demons? Can a human soul be possessed by evil spirits? Virtually every ancient religion in the world, including the Judeo-Christian tradition, affirms this awful reality. Some of us who scoffed at such possibilities from the standpoint of rationalism have had our thinking reversed by something more powerful than rationalism, personal experience with spiritual evil that defies all reason.[9]

In the Gospels, when Jesus exorcised a demon, the person got up and walked away whole. A dirty spirit had been in control of their true identity; when the spirit left, they returned immediately to their former, whole self. In other words, they repossessed their own soul.

> They came to the other side of the sea, to the country of the Gerasenes. And when he had stepped out of the boat, immediately a man out of the tombs with an unclean spirit met him. He lived among the tombs; and no one could restrain him any more,

even with a chain; for he had often been restrained with shackles and chains, but the chains he wrenched apart, and the shackles he broke in pieces; and no one had the strength to subdue him. Night and day among the tombs and on the mountains he was always howling and bruising himself with stones. When he saw Jesus from a distance, he ran and bowed down before him; and he shouted at the top of his voice, "What have you to do with me, Jesus, Son of the Most High God? I adjure you by God, do not torment me." For he had said to him, "Come out of the man, you unclean spirit!" Then Jesus asked him, "What is your name?" He replied, "My name is Legion; for we are many." He begged him earnestly not to send them out of the country. Now there on the hillside a great herd of swine was feeding; and the unclean spirits begged him, "Send us into the swine; let us enter them." So he gave them permission. And the unclean spirits came out and entered the swine; and the herd, numbering about two thousand, rushed down the steep bank into the sea, and were drowned in the sea. (Mk 5:1-13)

When the man got back to town, I wonder what he thought when he saw children playing. I imagine he smiled to see their games. For the first time in a long time, fun sounded fun.

The devil perhaps hates nothing more than innocent play. It must have sickened him to see David dance before the Lord with all his might (2 Sam 6:14). It vexes him when the saint proclaims: "You have turned my mourning into dancing; you have taken off my sackcloth and clothed me with joy" (Ps 30:11). The redeemed unconscious, determined to create, play and dance before the Lord, must be sorely lost territory for the evil one.

Whatever else it is, and whatever else it does, the greatest manifestation of the unconscious is its ability to create play, to feel joy and to worship God. These truest expressions of the human heart may be the reason Jesus tells us, "Truly I tell you, unless you change and become like children, you will never enter the kingdom of heaven" (Mt 18:3).

Four

Self-Portrait
in Ice Water

••••••••••••••••••••••••••••••••••••••

*T*wenty years ago a dachshund in a nursing home was a *wiener non grata;* today it is common for a canine healer to wander the halls of a convalescent hospital nuzzling up to patients. Patients loved by animals heal faster, live longer, are happier and probably complain less about the food.

Communication with animals is deeply human. It's good for us. We like to do it, and it is something we wish we could do better. It is so characteristically human to talk to animals that we worry about people who won't; we see them as less human, not more rational. A chat with a rock may indicate a mental dysfunction; never talking with animals may be just as serious a symptom. Horse trainers coo to their brutes. The best ranchers talk to their cattle, but the best farmers don't talk to their barley. The difference between talking to a cattail and talking to a fish may be no more than enzymes and body parts—or just maybe it is due to something beyond the arrangement of carbon atoms.

The simple observation that humans talk to animals by nature belies the difficult question why. The answer may be the Bible's teaching that animals have souls.

Animals and Souls

Does your dog have a soul? The Bible's answer to that question may surprise you. The account of the creation of Adam in Genesis 2 provides us with an intimate picture of the elements of human life: "And the LORD God formed man of the dust of the ground, and breathed into his nostrils the breath of life; and man became a *living soul*" (v. 7 KJV).

Dust, breathed into by God, makes Adam a living soul, in Hebrew *nephesh chayyah*. The Bible tells us that animals too have the breath of life, and they are *nephesh chayyah*.[1] Adam named the animals—presumably talking to them. The Hebrew text says that he named every *nephesh chayyah*. "So out of the ground the LORD God formed every animal of the field and every bird of the air, and brought them to the man to see what he would call them; and whatever the man called every *living creature*, that was its name" (Gen 2:19).

After the great flood, God made a covenant with Noah and with every *nephesh chayyah*, every descendant of every living creature that escaped the flood in the ark.

God said, "This is the sign of the covenant that I make between me and you and every *living creature* that is with you, for all future generations: I have set my bow in the clouds, and it shall be a sign of the covenant between me and the earth. When I bring clouds over the earth and the bow is seen in the clouds, I will remember my covenant that is between me and you and every *living creature* of all flesh; and the waters shall never again become a flood to destroy all flesh. (Gen 9:12-15)

One can hardly escape the inference that humanity and the animal kingdom are besouled by God and loved by God. Karl Barth says of animals: "According to the Old Testament, neither soul nor the Spirit can be simply denied the beasts."[2] Perhaps we talk to animals for the same reason we talk to each other: there is spiritual connection; living creatures relate to living creatures. The soul is relational, soul to soul, animal and human.

Love is a soul issue, and many of the higher animals exhibit love. C. S. Lewis, referring to a kind of love humans share with animals, says: "Nothing in Man is either worse or better for being shared with the beasts."[3] Do animals inherit eternal life? The inimitable George MacDonald gives us a hint of his dreams when he tells us, "I have a strong hope in my heart that the animals, too, are being taught for something higher and better."[4] Will there be animals in heaven? I hope so. Very often animals fill our experiences of heaven on earth.

Of Fishes, Midges and Rapture

In January on the Madison River in Montana, an aquatic insect about the size of a carrot seed hatches from its nymphal swimming stage on the bottom of the river into its adult flying stage. Fishers call the tiny creatures midges; entomologists call them *Chironomidaeis*. I've seen these crazy little bugs flying around in zero-degree air. They live most of their adult life in a microclimate, a half-inch blanket of warm air above the moving water.

Midges mate in this weather. Snowy weather gets them going. After mating, the female deposits eggs in the water; the eggs sink to the bottom of the river to begin the cycle anew.

"Mating" is a misnomer, because midges opt for orgies. They mass up, floating down the river in globs about the size of a chickpea. These spheres of gasping, grasping, groveling insects are more than trout can resist. So the trout rise, slurping them off the surface of the water.

It's fifteen degrees, and there's a ten-mile-an-hour wind blowing snow into my eyes. I'm up to my thighs in the Madison River, about thirty miles north of Yellowstone Park, dressed in neoprene chest-high waders and many layers of clothing. I must look like the Michelin Man. A herd of mule deer check me out. Some bighorn sheep ignore me, though the ram keeps an eye on me. I'm catching and releasing rainbow and brown trout, twelve to twenty inches in length, on dry flies—Parachute Adams, sizes

#18 to #24, for those interested.

The midges haven't massed together. The crazy fish are sipping individual flies off the surface. I haven't the slightest idea how they get enough nourishment from one of those little bugs to pay for the calories required to rise for them.

I flick ice off the chrome guides on my fly rod with my fingers, gingerly, remembering that I broke the tip off my new four-weight last year doing this very thing. My hands are cold, my feet are cramping up, and I am laughing loudly. This is marvel. The strike, the set, the line ripping off the reel, the fight—my soul giggles.

Fish slow down in cold water. In summer a large trout can rise through three feet of water, sip an insect off the surface of the water with almost no splash, and return to its holding water in a matter of two seconds. In winter trout porpoise slowly, almost painfully, breaking their own cardinal rule of survival: they expose much of their upper body rolling over their prey. The water seems thicker, almost oily. It sticks to the fish like caramel as they break the surface of the water. Everything is slo-mo.

The midges, zipping chaotically across the surface of the water, looking for love, seem as if they are on amphetamines. It's as if you are watching a video shot from an airplane flying over a small-town ice rink. People are skating, each to an individual pattern, but the patterns combine into a picture of random movements. Then someone hits the fast-forward button on the VCR. The skaters move at impossible speeds, with no apparent order, yet they don't crash into each other. That's what midges look like on a river in winter. Spring mayflies glide down the river like sailboats; midges look like a junior-high all-night party in a gymnasium.

The trout's world is slow-motion, the midge's world is fast-forward, but they meet. What the trout lacks in speed this time of year they gain in timing. Just as a slower basketball player with perfect timing can out-rebound a faster opponent, the trout's compensation for its slowed body functions makes the bout even. During heavy feeding the trout rise rhythmically, not wasting calories in jerky movements. They seem attached to wheels spinning slowly through the water. They rise to the clumps of midges floating on the current, but they also rise to sip the little zippers; somehow their rhythmic rise corresponds perfectly to the herky-jerky journey of the midges.

The nature of the trout's timed rise, and the tiny, flitting object of its desire, makes fishing a midge hatch one of the great challenges in dry fly-fishing. The flies must be small: as I said, #18s to #24s. You must cast the fly in the trout's face. This time of year they do not veer right or left. The fly must arrive in the trout's rise rhythm. Since each trout's rhythm is different, you must cast to one fish at a time.

When the fish sips the fly and the hook sets, the water explodes. An adrenaline rush overwhelms the fish's winter-slow metabolism. An awesome display of muscle, bone and fin ensues. One thing in the trout's favor is the higher percentage of dissolved oxygen in colder water. So the fish can fight. The increased oxygen helps it survive after it is released.

Many emotions surface as the trout gives out and you pull it up to your legs in the water. First there is delight. The animal is beautiful. Every winter fisher will tell you: winter enhances trout colors. Next comes sadness that the trout is defeated. I don't feel like a conqueror, just a person pulling some tricks to bring my shy friend close to me. Third, there is distaste. Releasing the fish makes my hands cold. The four great moments in fly-fishing are the strike, the fight, talking to the fish and watching it swim away. All fly-fishers talk to fish. I don't know a single one who doesn't. We talk to fish because they have souls.

Fly-fishing stinks as a religion, but it provides great religious experiences. It isn't just the fish, it isn't just the midges, it isn't just the snow, or the ice in the guides, or the numb fingers and the cramped toes. It's all of it. It is the beauty of the instant when all the parts—the zippy midges and the lethargic fish, slow, oily water exploding, the weight of the trout on the end of the line and the Hallelujah Chorus of trout colors—come together in a subjective experience of sheer wonder. It is the totality of it, the rapture of the moment in which every part, including me, becomes one and drowns and is reborn in beatific vision. If I wouldn't die of hypothermia, I'd fall on my face in the water and worship the God of heaven and earth with my whole body and my whole soul.

And yet that moment is a spark in the night compared to the revelation of heaven: "Then the angel showed me the river of the water of life, bright as crystal, flowing from the throne of God and of the Lamb" (Rev 22:1). That is the river my soul longs to see.

The reason fly-fishing is a lousy religion is that it fixes on the spark and ignores the flame. Seeing the spark, I long for the flame. Moses saw the flame in the wilderness, and out of that flame comes the secret of the human soul.

The Name of God and the Human Soul

In Hebrew, Greek and English, the word *soul* is a noun. But when *soul* gets stuck in the category of being a noun, we lose the essence of what the soul is and what we are. For whatever else it means to have a soul, it is more important that we *are* a soul—in other words, that we are alive.

Previously I said that the soul is "event-stuff," that it is continually generated by the Holy Spirit. This is admittedly difficult to think about. But we understand our life as an event. Within the one whole event we call our life, certain events stick out in our minds as defining ones. These events portray the essence of who we are and what our values are. Sometimes they cause such awe or horror that we never forget them. The soul is the spiritual, objective basis for the whole event of our life, and it is the spiritual, objective basis for the experience of the individual events that define and portray our lives.

The soul is more than just the human potential for spiritual experiences. The soul is our human, spiritual self in the very act of being. The soul is not a thing that acts. The soul exists in action. It is alive. It is "stuff" only to the extent that it is an "event." It is in the act of living that we are alive. We exist and we affirm our existence as living beings.

In this way the soul is made in the image of God. God is not thing, God is Person. God is the living God, the Person of the event of his own existence. God's existence in his personal nature as the living, powerful God is contained in his name. God's name in the Old Testament forces us to expand our understanding of nouns and verbs to account for a reality that is beyond both.

God revealed his name to Moses speaking from a burning bush.

God said to Moses, "I AM WHO I AM." He said further, "Thus you shall say to the Israelites, 'I AM has sent me to you.'" (Ex 3:14) God's name is a unique form of the Hebrew verb "to be." It obliterates our language's slavery to nouns and verbs, especially to nouns. The Jewish scholar Nahum Sarna says of the divine name: "Whatever the true etymology of the Tetragrammaton [the divine name], and to this day it remains an enigma, God's response to Moses' question . . . reflects a popular understanding that YHVH is to be interpreted in terms of the Hebrew stem h-y-h 'to be.'"[5] Roman Catholic scholar Roland de Vaux says the name can be paraphrased to mean "I am the Existing One."[6] Protestant scholar Gerhard von Rad would largely agree with Sarna and de Vaux. His assessment of the mystery of the name reminds one of what we sometimes try to do with the human soul: "But what is of greatest importance is that this name could not properly be objectified and disposed of."[7]

Sarna goes on to say about the name of God,

> Whether it means "I Am That I Am," or "I Am Who I Am," or "I Will Be What I Will Be," and it can mean any of these, God's pronouncement of God's Name indicates that He can be known only to the extent that he chooses to reveal His Self, and it can be truly characterized only in terms of itself, and not by analogy with something else. This is the articulated counterpart of the spectacle of the fire at the Burning Bush, the fire that is self-generating and self-sustaining.[8]

For all of its mystery, the divine name contains something extremely common to us. God says "I am." Don't we say this too?

God affirms his existence using a verb. We also affirm our existence with a verb. There is without question an absolute distinction between God's "I AM WHO I AM," in which he signifies his self-determined, eternal existence, and our puny "I am" in which we simply say almost in surprise, "I'm here and I'm alive." But the similarity is significant. The human affirmation "I am" is plenty mysterious and is, frankly, somewhat dangerous.[9] Our "I am" is not intended to be an affirmation of independent, eternal self-determination. It is, however, a legitimate, conscious, subjective affirmation of personal existence. In it we state the awesome truth that in some sense we exist in a way analogous to God.

Our affirmation of personal existence does not issue from our arms, our legs, our heart, our kidneys or even our brain. Somehow, something in us posits independent, subjective existence, and understands this independent subjective existence as the very nature and essence of our life. We can become quadriplegic and still maintain this stance in total. This independent, subjective existence evinces itself in our love and in our hate, in our grace and in our envy, in our peace and in our war. It manifests itself in the sinner's desperate attempt to be loose of God, and it evinces itself in the saint's desperate attempt to be lost in God.

Contained in the mysterious human affirmation "I am" is the secret of the soul. It manifests our identity and our subjectivity. It affirms that our existence is our life. We are not objects that act. Our objective reality exists in that we act. When we cease to act we are dead, no longer human, just corpses disintegrating into a few simple, atomic elements that trees and grass feed on. But our existence is not defined by the atoms that trees metabolize into bark.

The implications of this observation are enormous. One of the great riddles of spiritual existence is the paradox that we *cannot* be human without God (this is the insight of religion) but also that we *can indeed* be human without God[10] (this is the insight of atheism and agnosticism). The latter is a legitimate observation. We who are religious have failed miserably at admitting this. It hampers our evangelism, and our own spiritual quest.

The soul is continually breathed by the Holy Spirit. So it is true: we cannot exist without God. But the soul that is breathed by the Holy Spirit is so good and so powerful that we cannot deny that atheists, agnostics and people of all religions possess the power to create things that reveal goodness, truth and beauty.

That we can be human without God comes from our ability to say "I am." We can explore goodness, truth, beauty and even holiness on our own. In admitting this we take the soul's "I am" to its logical, if not its terrible, conclusion.

The Bible tells many stories in which a "righteous pagan" shows that he or she is very good, very faithful, and often more so than God's own people. Potiphar treated Joseph better than Joseph's own brothers did (Gen 39:1-6). Zipporah circumcised her son, saving Moses' life in the process (Ex 4:21-26). Jethro, Zipporah's father and Moses' father-in-law, gave Moses invaluable support and advice (Gen 18). Rahab saved the spies of Israel (Josh 2). Ruth was faithful to Naomi (Ruth 1). Uriah showed deep respect for his comrades in arms (2 Sam 11). Solomon imported an artisan from Tyre, Hiram, to do work in bronze for the temple (1 Kings 7:13). Naaman showed faith (2 Kings 5). The entire city of Nineveh repented (Jon 3). King Nebuchanezzar repented (Dan 4). King Cyrus allowed the Jews to return to their homeland and encouraged them to rebuild their temple (Ezra 1). King Xerxes (Ahasuerus) did not kill Queen Esther but listened attentively to her plea and believed her story (Esther 5). The Canaanite woman trusted Jesus completely to heal her daughter (Mt 15:21-28). A Roman centurion showed faith that surprised even Jesus (Mt 8:5-13). At the cross, when Jesus died, a centurion "praised God and said, 'Certainly this man was innocent' " (Lk 23:47) The Ethiopian eunuch was reading the Scriptures, eagerly seeking to know what they meant (Acts 8:26-40).

With the exception of the decree of King Cyrus, it appears from Scripture that God did not inspire the actions of these pagans. The plain sense of the text in every case is that they responded out of goodness in their own hearts.

Many people who do not know God are very good people. This

is a simple, straightforward deduction from the truth already stated: God made us good. Later we will deal with the fact that we all live in sinful rebellion against God. For now it is enough to say that we can create good things and exhibit goodness in our lives whether or not we acknowledge the existence of God who creates good. But our likeness to God positions us before him without excuse. Our likeness to God makes us responsible to God.

The soul is the subjective basis for our experience of wonder because the soul is itself a marvel. The soul is a treasure of possibility fueled by curiosity.

Curiosity

We care about truth because our soul cares about truth. Furthermore, the soul cares about truth that does not serve us directly or practically. We spend millions of dollars on telescopes to learn the secrets of the cosmos. We want to know how old the universe is, where it came from and where it is going. Why do we care about this? We don't know why we care about it. And we do not know why we cannot stop caring. But something tells us that if we stop caring about the origin and makeup of the universe, we will become much poorer. If we forbid science to continue learning about the universe, something spiritual in all of us will die.

How can this be? Our spiritual soul presses us to explore the material universe. Why should the spiritual soul care about the material universe? We can ask the same question of physicality. Why should a material being care about any material entity that contributes little or nothing to its well-being? There is no real reason why a pile of atoms should *care* about another pile of atoms. And frankly, just knowing that God created the universe does not explain why we care about it.

That we care to know the nature of the universe stems from a spiritual root in us, a similarity between us and the God who made it all. God cared to make the universe, and if we share a spiritual likeness to God it makes sense that we should care about the universe too. Traditional Judeo-Christian theology teaches that God created the universe out of nothing, under no compulsion from outside or within, but freely from the reservoir of his own love as an expression of joy. If God created the universe out of his own freedom, love and joy, what is human curiosity but our likeness to God in which we explore God's universe freely, lovingly and joyfully?

Scripture tells us that God determines the number of stars and calls each by name (Ps 147:4). Can there be any other reason that we name stars and birds, and that we cannot help but care how the stars are born and move, how birds fly and why a trout will rise in fifteen-degree air?

Basic curiosity drives the best science. Necessity may be the mother of invention, but curiosity is the genesis of attention. The best scientists are just a bunch of kids exploring our big back yard. By the way, why do children explore their back yard?

Curiosity is a self-propelling force. Wouldn't it be nice if we could stop pretending that we must care about truth for practical reasons, and just care to find the truth about things for the sake of finding the truth about things? When our daughter was a sophomore in high school she loved biology simply because it was interesting to her. She disliked history (which is interesting to me). From her perspective, once something has happened, so what? She delivered her postscript to her complaint about the study of history with a classic teenage eye roll: "The teacher says we need to study history so that we do not repeat the mistakes of the past."

As a lover of history I could only agree with her. I said, "The idea that we need to study the past so we don't make mistakes in the present is the lamest excuse for studying history ever invented. We study history just because we want to. That's the only good reason to study it." We care about the truth for the sole purpose of satisfying our souls.

Creativity

Creativity, the child of curiosity, is our ability to combine features of the universe around us into new thoughts, solutions, drawings, music, stories, poetry—you get the point: all forms of human creativity. In creating we gather what amounts to an infinite number of resources around us and in us, and we concoct new things.

Our body provides the soul with everything we can see, hear, touch and smell. Infinite variation begins even at the level of our body. Just as our fingerprints are different, our bodies are different throughout. We see, hear, touch and smell our environment differently. We do not see, hear, touch and smell things in the same order in our lives. We remember things differently. Our minds select and store memories of our infinitely different experiences in utterly unique ways. We each possess the possibility for creativity simply because we experience life so differently.

The world of the spirit compounds the variations. We all understand the words *father, mother, sister, brother, wife* and *husband* in unique ways. The spiritual communities we live in are different. Our bodies and their genetics are physical relations, but our interactions with one another—values, patterns of relations and histories—are things of the spirit.

The geography of the United States of America is the physical reality of the nation. Patriotism, insurgency and apathy are spiritual attitudes and relations to that physical reality. Two people on the same socioeconomic level, from the same racial group, within the same religious viewpoint, often value the United States of America differently.

And then there is the Person of God. What holds for the rest holds true for our relation and understanding of the Person of God. Every human being has some relation to God because we live in his universe, as creatures of his design, with souls breathed by his Spirit. How each of us lives in that relation and expresses that relation differs even within the same religion.

Our unconscious is packed with pictures and drives and fears and loves and all manner of spiritual reality sublime and horrid. Our mental processes juggle these realities, repressing some, recalling others, displacing drives upon various objects. This may be the origin of symbolism and perhaps even metaphor.

We choose the materials for our creations from what is available to us. As we have seen, however, what is available to us is not a limiting factor. To create a vessel to hold water, we choose from many different materials, with many different forms, for many different functions, to suit our many different tastes, based on our infinitely various physical abilities—strength, coordination, intelligence, skill acquisition and much more.

Our choice is a matter of will. But something even more wonderful than human will is involved in creativity. We enrich the process of creative synthesis with our ability to think in random patterns.

We possess the ability to see things and make things in patterns that have never existed before. We can gather materials and attitudes and patterns around a problem or a feeling and allow these materials, attitudes and patterns to interact randomly until a "fit" occurs and things not correlated before come together in a unique creation. Every human being can do this and does do this. For example, no two sentences, spoken, written or recited, are ever written or vocalized in precisely the same way. If they were, Shakespeare's plays would have been performed only once.

Every morning is new, and each day provides new ways to say "I love you." For every idea and for every feeling as many similes and metaphors exist as there are fish in the sea. We need simply cast the line. The creation of beauty is an ever-new, inexhaustible possibility for the human race forever.

Beauty requires order, randomness and radiance. Everything beautiful communicates radiance. Radiance is the personal glory of the creator expressing itself through the object of beauty and striking the perceiver as praiseworthy. Everything beautiful has order. Every sentence has a beginning and an end, even if the speaker was born talking and didn't stop until he or she died. Leaves fall down, not up. Warm air rises, cold air sinks. We value symmetry, but we do not worship it. Leaves fall and winds shift in unpredictable patterns, obeying "laws" of "chaos" that we are only beginning to fathom and that are vital to beauty.

Every beautiful thing has some randomness. How dreadful it would be if mountains were perfectly shaped triangles! It would be grotesque if needles fell from trees in a specific direction, or if leaves fell in stacks. What if all people looked exactly the same? *That* would be an oppressive world.

I believe this profound feature of humanness is a function of the soul. Certainly the process takes place in our conscious and unconscious minds, since once we lose these functions to, say, a stroke, we lose the ability to be creative, and severely mentally retarded persons are not creative people. Nevertheless, when everything is in place and the creative act occurs, it is not so much an act of the body, or the brain, or even the conscious or unconscious mind. Creativity is in its deepest essence a product of the soul.

The creative act is our own way of saying "I am." It reflects who we are, what we are. Creative worship is our own gift to God. Creative gift giving is our own response to our dear other. We value our best creative acts with distinctly divine spiritual values.

As the apostle Paul tells us, "Finally, beloved, whatever is true, whatever is honorable, whatever is just, whatever is pure, whatever is pleasing, whatever is commendable, if there is any excellence and if there is anything worthy of praise, think about these things" (Phil 4:8). Creativity is not the process of trying to define the one right way to do something. There are innumerable ways to raise children right, and innumerable ways to raise them wrong. There are innumerable ways to do a little bit of both—which is closer to what actually happens. There are innumerable ways to raise children fostering goodness, truthfulness, holiness and beauty. There are infinite numbers of ways to tell a child you love them and infinite numbers of way to teach a child you hate them.

The challenge is to synthesize every factor in the creative process with truth, goodness, beauty and holiness. These are not moral absolutes. They are attributes of God. The soul knows them, absorbs them, sees them and creates new things with them because the soul—our irreducible, spiritual center—is breathed by God. Values like beauty and goodness and truth and holiness are not peripheral to us; they are central to what it means to be human. They are central to what it means that we are living souls living in a world filled with living souls, animal and human.

Part 2

The Soul
at Work

••

Five

Beauty

Shimmering Spirit

••

But a stream would rise
from the earth,
and water the whole face
of the ground.
GENESIS 2:6

*R*ing. Ring.

My shoulders sink, my face grimaces. Another interruption.
This better be something good.

"Hello."

"May I speak with the pastor, please?"

"Yeah, this is the pastor; what can I do for you?"

"Pastor, I'm calling today from Christian Family Productions
in Awe-stin, Te-xis. Pastor, could I have a few minutes of your
time this afternoon so that I could describe our newest video
series, Raising Rover the Bible Way? [Before I can answer:]
Pastor, Raising Rover the Bible Way is a new video series on dog
training using biblical principles, especially designed for use by
single-parent families. I'm sure you agree, pastor, that training a
dog is particularly difficult for single parents . . ."

"You know, I just don't have time this afternoon . ."

"It will only take a few minutes, pastor, and today I can offer you two series for the price of one. Today only, I can send you Ripping Your Child's Ego to Shreds the Bible Way, free with your purchase of Raising Rover the Bible Way. Pastor, does that make this offer more appealing to you?"

"We ordered one video series from you three years ago, and we have never used it. Please take our church's name and phone number off your list."

"Thank you for your time this afternoon, pastor; have a good day."

Click.

First it was "the pastor's study," then it became "the pastor's office"; now it's "shipping and receiving." What am I doing sitting in this stupid office on a gorgeous October afternoon anyway? I'm outta here.

Escape

So I grab my book, my reading glasses, a pen and a yellow underliner and walk home. I load up my old orange Vanagon with a lawn chair and my fishing stuff and head out of town to a spring creek five minutes from my office. Here the water flows naturally and generously, bubbling up out of the ground.

When I arrive I can see from my car window that the fish are rising.

A hatch! I've hit it!

I get my stuff on, string up my rod, tie on a new tippet and a fly, and I'm off to the races. The spring creek is crystal clear, slow glassy water, and the fish scare easily, but that doesn't daunt me today.

I cast and cast, move ahead and cast some more, and the fish scatter before me like the sunbathers used to at San Clemente when I'd bring a group of forty-five junior-highers to the beach. Those poor people would watch with terror as I decided where I'd put my towel down. "Please God, not here!" they'd cry.

So I put all the fish in the creek down. I go back to the van, set up my lawn chair facing northeast, so the sun and the creek are at my back, and pull out my book, *Spirit and Beauty* by Patrick Sherry.

The presence of God's beauty in the world is often expressed metaphorically. Hopkins' line "The world is charged with the grandeur of God" is one which sticks in the mind, and the next line "It will flame out, like shining from shook foil" introduces the theme of light . . .[1]

A high-pitched, ridiculous "gurgle! gurgle! gurgle!" diverts my attention to the thick red willows behind me. Sandhill cranes. Funny-sounding birds. They are big. In a field, from a distance, they look like deer. Back to the book.

Jonathan Edwards combines the theme of light with the metaphor of reflection when he says that God is to be loved because He is "infinitely the most beautiful and excellent: and all the beauty to be found throughout the whole creation, is but the reflection of the diffused beams of that Being who hath an infinite fullness of brightness and glory."[2]

What Is Beauty?

I close the book briefly to think about what I just read.

I still can't believe I spent fifty bucks on this skinny little book, I think. But I'm really glad I bumped into it in St. Paul. My concentration is shot. But it is interesting reading . . .

The cognate of a mirror is also common: in one of his sonnets Michelangelo says that he will only love human beauty because it mirrors God.[3]

Plip.

Water sound. Behind my back. Bet it's a muskrat.

Plip. Plip.

That's no muskrat. Fish are sipping behind me. Rotating slowly, I see rings in the flat water.

A fish ten yards downstream nipples the surface, a tiny disturbance causing a ring of energy to flow out across the water. From here you can't tell if the fish is four inches or twenty inches.

How about getting my gear together and fishing? No, instead of indulging in predation, I'll worship.

I turn back in my chair, facing the valley.

Plip. Plip. Plip.

The spring creek snakes its way through a hay field. The Bridger Range starts five or six miles east of here. They sweep up forty-five hundred feet above the Gallatin Valley. The first of the winter snowpack dusts the upper half. I breathe deeply and exhale slowly. This is such a beautiful place. Why do I notice the beauty sometimes but not every time? Maybe the question isn't what beauty is. Maybe the question is, why do I see it? Why do I feel it? Why do I see it and feel it at certain times and not others?

I turn to the creek. It's about twenty-five feet wide and six inches to three feet deep. There's lots of weeds, some rocks and too much silt.

Plip. Plip. Plip.

I focus on the fish. There's probably twenty rising. Never at once. One here, one there, across the stream, up close. The fish rise in a rhythm orchestrated by their metabolism and their reaction to the patterns of the flies on the surface of the stream. Taken as a whole, the fish are rising in a random pattern. This causes the rings of energy that flow outward from the rise to meet in ever-changing, unpredictable patterns.

I often think how dreadful it would be if rivers cut straight canyons or if clouds were square. How horrid a world we would live in without random patterns! We would feel trapped at every turn.

But like the fish rising, and the midges zipping, and the creek snaking and the mountains rising, things happen in patterns unpredictable and unfathomable. That is a lot of what beauty is about. Is God like that? Is God, who is immortal, invisible, unhasting and unchanging, also unpredictable? The Psalms tell us that God has placed the stars in place. I believe this. Did he sprinkle them? Does he set it up so that things will take their place in an order unthinkable, unpredictable and therefore grand because he is a God of love and love gives freedom?

Watching the Trout
One fish catches my eye. It is occupying a favored position in the stream, so it probably is a big one. It is rising right up against a

deep-cut bank in about three feet of water. The fish is stationary in a depression in the bank, with a spit of grass and sticks forming a little point on the upstream side. This makes the water coming downstream collect before the spit and speed up as it clears the spit and pushes past the depression.

The trout lies in the dead water of the depression, tangential to the faster water speeding off the spit. This gives the trout the benefit of not having to move. (Trout are lazy.) Since it is near a cut bank, it can disappear very quickly. (Trout are insecure.) And the faster-moving water brings more feed by. (Trout are greedy.)

This beauty is rising on my side of the creek about forty feet downstream from me. My guess is that the fish is about fourteen to eighteen inches long. I can't tell yet if it is a rainbow or a brown. I think it may be a brown; big browns tend to lie near the bank. They tend to be solitary. Rainbows feed in groups, or "pods" as we call them.

Slowly I move to the car and get out my binoculars. I crawl on hands and knees to the bank and find a comfortable place to sit in the grass, hoping, trusting that the trout will not see me, or in any case not care about me. I want to watch this one. The fish is just far enough away for the binoculars to focus. I feel very lucky. I can practically see its teeth when it rises, opens its mouth and sips a fly! Big teeth. Must be a brown.

A "hatch" is when aquatic insects rise from their liquid home for an extremely short adult life span in open air, usually less than twenty-four hours, in order to mate. Today the hatch is an assortment of mayflies. I don't know their scientific names, but some are blue-gray and some are a light brown color. With the binoculars I can see them emerge to the surface of the water and pop out of their casings. It's like watching a chick hatch from an egg. The bug struggles to push its wings up, and then it glides down the stream on the surface tension of the water, drying its wings so it can fly away to mate. These are called "duns." After the flies mate, the females deposit the fertilized eggs in the water. They die on the water, and their wings, no longer upright, lie spread-eagled on the water's surface. These are called "spinners."

Sometimes the fish take the "emergers," the insects swimming to the surface and popping out of their casings. Sometimes they take duns. Sometimes they take spinners. Very often they feed on all three. Today, though, they seem to be slurping duns off the surface.

Trout rarely jump in a spring creek. They jump in fast water so that they can overcome the speed of the water. In a creek like this one, where the water is very slow and flat, they simply twist their fins up, rise slowly and take flies right off the surface with little disturbance or effort. Remember: trout are lazy and insecure.

With my binoculars I watch the place where the big trout is hanging out. I'm facing west, and the afternoon sun is putting an orange sheen on the water, so I can't see the fish, but the light makes the insects stand out like circus performers.

The flies scatter unevenly across the water at about three per square foot of water surface. When they hit the little spit of grass and sticks, they bunch up and speed up into the trout's feeding lane.

Here's my game: Which bug will the trout take? The biggest one? Any bug that floats right over its snout? What rhythm will the trout adopt?

The trout may or may not take the biggest flies. Trout don't "think" about bugs. They rise on instinct. Their instincts key them to the numbers of bugs as well as sizes of bugs. Generally, there are more small insects than large ones. This means that usually the fish will see more small bugs than large ones. So will the fish take the more numerous smaller insects or the less numerous but more juicy larger ones? It also depends on how particular the fish wants to be. Sometimes fish will take anything that looks buggy on the surface of the water. At other times they will take only one type of insect, one size, one color, one stage. Sometimes there will be flies all over the stream, but the fish will be feeding only on the blue-gray ones of a certain size as they are emerging. The rest they leave alone. At other times they feed on anything. Why? I haven't got the slightest idea.

Well, anyway, this trout seems to be in a happy-go-lucky mood.

He's taking different sizes and colors of duns. He doesn't seem to be interested in the emergers, just the duns. That makes it fun, because I can see what he's taking.

The water is quiet, with an orange glint. The duns perch on its surface tension like birds on a wire. When will he rise? Where exactly? Which fly will trigger his instinct?

There is a slight swell of water, followed by the "lips" breaking the surface; the mouth is open, the water flows into the mouth—and out the gills—and a fly goes right down the gullet. The fish continues with an arced follow-through. I see the eyes, then the dorsal fin and the thickly muscled back. The rear emerges with a snap and the trout disappears. When will it rise again? Which fly will it take? What is this fish's rhythm?

I wait about ten seconds, then pick out a medium-sized blue-gray dun twenty feet upstream from the spit; I think it will hit the spit and float by the fish in the right position at the right time.

This is more than a game. It's practice. These are the kinds of calculations I would have to be making if I were trying to catch this fish.

The fly follows the path I foresaw. It hits the spit at the right place and spins off into the feeding lane at the right time. I see the water swell, a second early; the trout takes a much smaller fly. Try again.

This time I choose one a bit smaller, still blue-gray, in the same place on the water. The dun heads toward the spit, but when it arrives it catches a subsidiary current and spins outside the feeding lane, into the main current. I watch it for a while as it runs the gauntlet of trout in the middle. This one may live to mate.

Another fly. Same position. Same size and color. It hits the spit right, speeds into the feeding lane. The trout, hidden for about twenty seconds, emerges; but it shifts left and guzzles down a large, dusky brown mayfly outside of what I thought was its feeding lane. Why? Big fly? Dusky color? A whim?

Now I get less calculating in choosing my fly. I peruse a general area, pick a general fly and watch it float downstream into the feeding lane and down the fish's gullet. Wow. I love this better than fishing. Does that mean I'm going to give up fishing? No.

I want to see the fish better. So I crawl "down crick," away from the bank, and creep through the tall grass, avoiding bovine deposits as best I can, to the place where I think the fish is working. The grass is high enough that I have to stand to see it. Slowly, I mean really . . . slowly . . . I stand up and peer over the bank to see the fish, now six feet from my nose. It's a rainbow, about seventeen inches. It shoots like a cruise missile upstream and under the bank.

Shoot. I blew it. I couldn't resist seeing it up close. Now it's gone. Usually when you "put a fish down" like this, it's gone for good. And the other fish saw me too. They're all down now.

So I go back to my lawn chair. My watch says 3:30. Whew, I watched that fish for forty minutes. I pick up *Spirit and Beauty* . . .

It is perhaps easier to express the relationship between God's glory and earthly beauty poetically and metaphorically than to attain any philosophical or theological exactitude. Hence prudence might suggest that we stop at this point.[4]

Spring Creeks

A hundred sandhill cranes fly low over my head. They'd gleaned from a harvested wheat field across the creek, over the willows in the next ranch. It's as if the sky were filled with gray-brown deer—they are so big! They look awkward on land, but they fly in magnificent sync. A multitude of heavenly hosts cries: "Gurgle! Gurgle! Gurgle!" My eyes lift off the page toward the sky, to the Bridgers. That's where the spring creek comes from.

I guess I haven't even said what a spring creek is. A spring creek is a stream of water that emerges from underground. It doesn't start in the mountains like normal streams and rivers, drip merging with drip, rivulets flowing together to form creeks, meeting to make streams that merge into rivers. A spring creek starts in the mountains, like regular streams, but instead of flowing above ground the water goes underground, sinking into rock fields, decomposed granite and sand, and these strata often reach down into the valley. The water flows down of course, through the permeable layers, into the valley, filling the valley's water table.

Now if you drill a well, in some places you hit water at a hundred feet, but the water in the well might rise up to within four feet of the well cap. The water is under some pressure. Not a lot, but some. Well, if a water-bearing stratum of sand or gravel is exposed at the surface of the ground, then that water will flow out of the ground all by itself. That is a spring creek.

A spring creek is special trout habitat because the water stays at essentially the same temperature all year around. It doesn't get too warm for the trout in the summer, and it doesn't freeze up in winter. It's good for bugs too. The water picks up nutrients on its trip from the mountains to the surface as it seeps through the limestone-laced Gallatin Valley. This fecund water is ideally suited for microorganisms, plants, bugs and trout.

Ranchers love spring creeks. They provide water for cattle all winter long. During hot summers they rarely go dry.

Ancient peoples loved spring creeks too. The residents of Palestine called them "living water."

This spring creek serves many functions. The rancher irrigates with it, his cattle drink from it year round, and the fish like it too. This creek is good fishing. Over in Livingston, Montana, about forty-five minutes away, a few awesome spring creeks attract fly fishers from all over the world to the tune of fifty bucks a day.

Back to *Spirit and Beauty:*

But philosophers and theologians have attempted to go further, so we must follow them and try to assess their attempts. The simplest and most common version of the idea which we are exploring . . .[5]

Good. Probably the simple one is the only one I will be able to understand. I'd better pay attention.

. . . to be found among philosophers and theologians is that worldly beauty is like God's beauty because God has communicated a likeness of His own beauty; and that there are degrees of likeness to God according to the extent that creatures share in the communication, resulting in a hierarchy of beauty.[6]

That makes me think of the human body, though I'm the only human around. I look up to the Bridgers. The late afternoon sun is putting a pink tint on them now.

Water Living and Light

Plip. Plip. Plip.

The trout are rising again. I turn around, and guess what: that trout is back in its place, sipping flies. I return to the grassy spot, but without the binoculars. The sun has lit the water on fire. The rising trout have created energy waves that meet and contradict and flow together, creating a random ripple effect on the water. The ripples pick up the late October sun and shimmer with pink and orange and gold and silver. It is as if the trout were feeding on light.

I am no longer fixed on the trout. I am just flat-out worshiping God.

"Lord, this is beautiful. Just beautiful. It is a reflection of your glory."

I can't help but think of Revelation 4:

Coming from the throne are flashes of lightning, and rumblings and peals of thunder, and in front of the throne burn seven flaming torches, which are the seven spirits of God; and in front of the throne there is something like a sea of glass, like crystal. (vv. 5-6)

And I flash to Christ, the living water and the light of the world, the metaphors merged here. Is this not a reflection of his glory?

Then I get cognitive. I don't really want to, but there the thought is.

Is this creek the *highest* form or reflection of God's beauty? Is this creek the image of God?

Sherry says, "There are degrees of likeness to God according to the extent that creatures share in the communication, resulting in a hierarchy of beauty."[7]

As I watch the display of lights and life on the spring creek, I wonder if the human body is not a higher form of the likeness of God, even more beautiful than this.

I think of a conversation I had with a photographer.

Beauty and Soul

I had to get a picture taken. After the photographer finished the noxious task, I pointed at some fashion magazines he had displayed, and asked him: "What makes a woman beautiful? Why, for instance, are these women so beautiful? What makes them that way?"

The photographer smiled appreciatively. "That's a good question. You know, I have never photographed a woman who wasn't beautiful—or *any* person, male or female, who wasn't beautiful. I really haven't," he declared with certainty.

"What do you mean by that?" I said.

"When I photograph, my goal is to bring the true person out in the picture. These models are beautiful because somehow they can communicate something very special about themselves through their faces and their bodies. That's what I try to bring out in a picture: the true self. When that happens, the picture is always beautiful."

"So in a sense, what you try to do is draw out the person's soul, their inner self, and make it radiate through their body."

"Yes, that's what I try to do," he agreed.

"So the beauty is in the body and the soul, and particularly in the soul radiating through the body."

"Yeah, that's right. That's what I mean." He was still smiling.

As I continue to look at the spring creek and the fires of the sun dim, the water turns a dark gray-green. I feel the beauty of this moment in my soul. Maybe if the photographer were here to take a picture of me as I watch the fireworks on the water, my face would glimmer with light—not just the light reflecting off the water, but light from within my soul, working its way out through my body, making me into a bright image of God. And maybe God likes it that way. Perhaps my delight in the moment is nothing compared to his.

Six

Goodness

Bicycle Bob &
Albert Einstein

●●

*F*rom its severe southern angle, the winter afternoon sun shot through the dry, frigid mountain air and burned directly into the white linen curtains covering the sanctuary's huge side windows, saturating the room with bone-warming, radiant heat and a brilliant white light that produced no shadows. As the room filled with nervous people shuffling quietly into their seats, I paced the floor in a back room like a midge skating madly on ice water.

"Pray for me," I said to one of the musicians in an agitated voice. "I don't know if I can pull this off."

"I'm sure it will be fine," a kind voice reassured me, hoping no doubt to calm my jangled nerves, and perhaps hers as well.

This would not be a good funeral to blow. The little guy was one of the town's most beloved figures.

As I wore the carpet out, I mumbled key lines, fumbled with my canary-colored notes and saw the man alive—his inimitable figure moved clear-cut in my mind. I saw him riding his bike to town.

I can't say this ... it is totally ridiculous. I'm making a mockery of one the great men of the town, I told myself, letting my fear interrupt my vision. But practical reality hog-tied my fear: two minutes is not enough time to prepare a new sermon. I would have to take the leap. *Lord, you loved this man; be faithful not to me but to him in what I say.*

A Soul in Sunlight

Driving south on Highway 93, I passed him along the road nearly every weekday morning at about the same time. I ripped down the road at sixty miles per hour; he wobbled in the same direction on his bicycle, all knees and elbows, struggling desperately to ride on the white line marking the boundary of the highway and the shoulder. His front wheel jiggled back and forth. He swerved onto the highway, then over the line onto the paved shoulder, onto the decomposed-granite gravel shoulder and almost into the ditch; then, overcorrecting himself, he swerved back onto the highway.

"We were afraid of him when we were children." A voice interrupted my mental video; it was another of the musicians. "He looked real scary, but after a while we realized that he was a kind man, and we all grew to love him.

"All us kids called him Bicycle Bob; the whole town called him that," she finished.

"Uh-huh," I answered.

I remembered his herky-jerky figure black from the back. Since for most of the year the sun comes from the south, what I saw was his shadow side as we headed south down the highway to town. The morning sun blasting the valley's thin, dry air made the snow-capped Bitterroots to the west shine and laid a soft amber glow on the grain and hay fields below them. The rolling, deep-wooded, shaded Sapphire Mountains lay to the east. They seemed cold.

I always wondered if I was going to hit him when I passed him on the highway. And I always looked at his face as I cleared him. It reflected torture. With dead earnest, real fear, dread determination and angry frustration, he made the trip every day from his shack north of town to his people in town, with no doubt about his need to make the trip.

I looked at my watch. 1:00 p.m. Dead on. "Let's go for it," I said to my little troop of musicians and worship assistants. The ladies preparing the meal for after the service wished us well. I turned the black porcelain knob, forcing the squeaky, ninety-year-old door past the place where it sticks, and we entered the sanctuary.

My throat constricted as I saw the room packed fuller than any time since Alice's funeral. Every powerful person in town had showed up. The retired community had come, as had every working person who could get the time off. They came to honor Bob. They had known him intimately for sixty years. And I who had known him peripherally for seven years was going to sum up his life in one potentially absurd analogy. During the few seconds I sat in the pulpit chair waiting for the prelude music to end, I saw the man alive again.

I was sitting across the table from him at the senior citizens' lunch. His greasy salt-and-pepper hair went every which way. His face began late off a very low forehead, and his bronzy, leathery, wrinkled, scrunched face moved all over as he chomped his food. His large, coated tongue moved in and out of his mouth. God only knows how he avoided masticating it into hamburger. He talked and chewed and swallowed and put more food in his mouth in a seamless act.

He had his own language, most of which was English, though I think there was some Crow mixed in, and I honestly think he was easiest to understand when he was talking with a mouth full of food. He talked about life and people and the government, telling jokes, pointing out ironies, carrying on a rural can-you-top-this conversation with himself. Always there was the open-throated laughter.

Silly me wondered if he'd choke on his beans and wienies. The people loved him. And he loved them. He made his deadly trip each day because he needed them, but I think he also knew that they needed him. They needed his smiles and his jokes and his smokes shooting through his disability. The light of his soul overwhelmed the darkness of his physical existence. He gave his gift for free.

I gazed at the crowd. I probably looked angry. There were some rascals there, people shipwrecking their lives on the reef of common sense and common morality. It struck me that if they had as much moral bearing as Bob, they'd all be as rich and as happy as they thought they deserved to be.

During the resolution chord of the prelude I saw Bob again. He was outside the Senior Center after lunch, standing in the gravel parking lot, sun in his face, in the middle of people, slowly dragging on a cigarette that hung from his smiling lips. As he talked, the cigarette dipped toward the earth like a lucky water witch. The smoke and the sun made him squint. This was the best time of the day for Bob. This was why he came to town. He could have eaten at home. He could have had Meals on Wheels. The county home-health nurses would have seen to it, and there would have been no shortage of volunteers to bring him food. However, with his friends, laughing at jokes only he completely understood, he stood as a free man, with dignity. This dignity was the reason he risked his life every day to come to town.

In Praise of Goodness

Once the service started, I got caught up in it and forgot my nervousness. We read Scriptures, prayed and heard a beautiful testimony of Bob's life by the Senior Center cook. Then it was my turn.

As I rose to speak, I think my face flushed. I stood in the pulpit checking my notes to see that they were in the right order, killing time, waiting for my spirit to settle down. For one last moment I considered chucking my notes and winging it. Then I saw him again, his eyes sparkling through his smoke and a huge, broad smile dissecting his square, flat face. I knew I had to take the risk.

God, this is dumb, I said to myself. I turned it into a prayer: *Lord, help me.*

I opened my Bible and read the text: "Blessed are the meek, for they will inherit the earth" (Mt 5:5). The text and the vision gave me the courage to proceed.

"This afternoon I would like to talk to you about the similarities between Bicycle Bob and Albert Einstein."

I paused and looked for their reaction. It was too late to turn back, but I wanted to know if my ship was sunk. Most looked interested; several were blank-faced. A few faces beamed; their eyes said that they could get up right now and preach the sermon for me. Energy poured into my body.

"I know the suggestion may sound ridiculous, but there are more similarities between the two than you might think. For instance, Bicycle Bob and Albert Einstein both had hair that went all different directions, and they didn't seem to care. Both of them were members of a persecuted people. Albert Einstein was a Jew and Bicycle Bob was part Indian. Both Bicycle Bob and Albert Einstein spoke their own language which few understood. Bicycle Bob and Albert Einstein were both of stellar moral character, and though neither was a confessing Christian, I wonder if they do not now live in the presence of the merciful and loving God, and if in the resurrection of the dead, they will enjoy eternal life fully restored. The dissimilarity of their mental abilities was less than the similarity of their moral natures.

"Moral bearing is not a function of intelligence. Bob's mental retardation and his physical disabilities did not affect his inner goodness. He had a tough upbringing and he lived a hard life, but he was a good man, a lot better man than many others with greater advantages. His goodness came from his soul, just as Albert Einstein's goodness came from his soul. Their brains worked differently, but their souls worked alike.

"Being a good man has little to do with being a smart man. If goodness came from intelligence, there would be more good people in the world. Instead the problem we face is that there are far more intelligent people in the world than there are good people in the world. Why?

"Goodness makes sense. Listen to the words of the apostle Paul on love: 'Love is patient; love is kind; love is not envious or boastful or arrogant or rude. It does not insist on its own way; it is not irritable or resentful; it does not rejoice in wrongdoing, but rejoices in the truth. It bears all things, believes all things, hopes all things, endures all things' (1 Cor 13:4-7).

"Why is this so complicated? How would your family life be different if you were patient? How many more friends would you have if you were kind? How much happier would you be if you were not envious of those around you? You know good and well how important it is to your business for you not to be arrogant or rude. Wouldn't this be a much better world if we didn't insist on our own way?

"It doesn't take a genius to figure out that good living improves our lives and the lives of those around us. Bob didn't even know the definition of some of these words, but he lived this way. What made him so smart? His soul was smart. His mind couldn't define goodness, but his soul lived in it, and the goodness in his soul permeated his whole life.

"One man was a genius, one man was mentally retarded, but both lived good lives. Both had good souls."

Of Moral Retardation

The congregation loved it.

All along I had hoped the talk would be fun for them. However, as I came to the end there was a blow to deliver, and I was chickening out. As I finished my sermon with the front of my mind, the back of my mind evaluated whether I should deliver the final, fateful lines.

I saw his face again. If I failed, Bob's life and his daily sacrifice on the highway might go unfulfilled. I saw him again, grinning with half-chewed food hanging out of his mouth. I decided to take the risk. In went the final nail.

"Bob was *mentally* retarded, but he was not *morally* retarded," I said slowly and deliberately.

I stopped to let it sink in, then I repeated myself.

"Let me say that again. Listen to me now. Bob was *mentally* retarded, but he was not *morally* retarded. Don't weep for Bob. Weep for those with perfect intelligence who are morally re-tarded. They are the ones in trouble. Sometimes I think I would like to quit this job and work with mentally retarded people. It would have to be easier than working with morally retarded people."

I stopped and looked at the congregation face by face, into each pair of eyes, into each skull, into each soul, with a very long pause.

One by one they took the hush inward. Conviction of sin settled onto the crowd like a wave of overpowering depression, as together and individually they realized that Bob's life had testified against theirs for sixty years.

Seven

Truth

Perfect Pitch

●●

*B*acking down the driveway, he pinched the little black box and the garage door closed. He wondered: if he didn't close the door, maybe someone would steal their stuff and they could avoid the yard sale. It would be a tough thirty-minute drive to the church. After worship the congregation would meet. He faced a no-confidence vote. This was not his first. He'd won some and lost some, but this time he knew the odds were against him.

What hurt most was looking over at his wife. She'd endured these like a trooper for over twenty-five years since he got fired from that first youth pastorate. She'd stick with him, of course, but the affection had worn thin over the years. She couldn't figure out why things always turned out bad for him. He had talent. He was a good preacher. He had good ideas. He was musical. He really did care about people. At first she blamed the churches. Now she knew something was wrong with him.

Yesterday, sitting on his sunny deck, he figured out that somewhere around his fifteenth year in ministry she had changed her mind. That was when she'd realized that it wasn't always the church's fault. He respected her for facing the truth. He knew she was right; he just didn't know what he could do about it. The changes he needed to make, which would have been easy for her, were impossible for him. That was where the tension lay between them. In the long run, her blaming him for his failures made it easier on him. He accepted blame from certain people, including her, readily. It hurt him when she spoke against the church. He owed a lot to the church.

For all the troubles over all the years, he could look back and see a lot of good he'd done. He'd built some church buildings in the fifties and sixties. He'd guided some small, struggling churches to financial stability. He'd led people to Christ. Heck, he still got missionary letters from kids he'd led to Christ in that youth group twenty-five years ago. Fantastic Christians. That was the kind of stuff that kept him going. But everywhere he went, it seemed like there were two or three families, or a cadre of retired people, that he'd knock heads with.

He couldn't sluff off the slams. The criticisms, normal stuff over minor things, ate him up inside. He'd line himself up against his detractors. He knew he shouldn't hate, but he couldn't talk himself out of, or pray himself out of, or discipline himself out of, the inner acid. He'd set the Pharisees up for a confrontation, and then his fatal flaw, his purple temper and red-hot tongue, would strike. That was when the support from the majority disappeared. The line on him at denominational headquarters was (according to his friend on the inside) "Great talent, fatal flaw."

As he drove, some violent motion caught his eye. His head jerked right and he looked through the window, past his wife's shoulder. He saw a park. In the park a child was running from a man. The child was running the opposite direction the car was traveling, so his eyes followed the child by looking through the right rear window; this made his wife shift uncomfortably, as she felt some danger of the car going out of control. The man caught the boy, popped him one across the head and dragged him back to what appeared to be a family picnic.

That was the last he remembered of the drive to the church. He didn't remember getting on the Santa Ana Freeway, getting off at Harbor Boulevard or anything else of the route to the church, with the exception of a billboard here and there.

Danny Boy

He was back in Havre, Montana, in the thirties, about seven years old, sitting at a corner table in a bar, waiting for his dad to finish his nightly gig. A few well-dressed young couples from Butte had finished dinner and were still drinking beer, listening to his dad. Their table was close to his, and they spoke loudly.

"Where'd a dumb, ugly Norwegian learn to play and sing like that?" said one of the men.

"He's not dumb, and not ugly either; anyway, he sings like a god," retorted the lady next to him.

Another man leaned back in his chair, cocked his head up and tugged on his chin, preparing his audience for professorial satire. He proposed the only possible explanation.

"There's never been a Norwegian born to a woman that can hit *any* note, let alone have pitch and timbre like this man. What we have here is not a freak of nature, but a genetic peculiarity. He must be part Irish."

His friends beamed, enjoying every syllable. He became dramatic.

"A Viking, a thousand years ago, snagged a wench off the Irish coast and brought her home to his fjord in Norway, where she bore him children. What you see here is her offspring, the poor woman resurrected, and tonight we vindicate her honor."

They were sitting near the wood stove, and it popped and hissed loudly. The professorial man leaned forward over the table and said in dead earnest, "I swear to God, this man has perfect pitch." Then, exploding backwards in his chair, he exclaimed, "And only the Irish have perfect pitch."

"Indeed!" they shouted, and they raised their mugs to such a beautifully self-evident truth.

When Dad hit the opening for "Danny Boy," the boy knew the shift was nearly over. He felt relief and some fear. The saloon owner ordered Dad to sing "Danny Boy" whenever the crowd included people with money who might be from Butte. He ordered him to sing it last, because he knew the out-of-town train travelers expected it and would drink while they waited.

While he sang, the young couples sat in silent rapture, tears sloshing in their eyes. Afterward, as they finished their beers, they cried and cried and cried, which really embarrassed the boy, and they clinked their mugs over and over to ancestors and famines and boats and mines and unions. They left happily, with their world quite in order.

When they got back to their room, Dad smacked him a few good ones and sent him to bed. Dad finished the night in the bottle he'd bought with tips from the young couples.

He hadn't remembered that night for a long time. He vaguely remembered Dad's drinking, but the other side of Dad's life, a better side, was much clearer to him.

He must have been twelve or thirteen when he and Dad wandered into a Methodist church in Great Falls on a Sunday night for a revival. After the music, some of which Dad liked and some of which made him cringe, an old preacher stepped up into the pulpit. His leathery-brown face held eyes that blazed like acetylene torches. In his introductory remarks he told the hundred or so present that as a young man he'd been converted at a revival preached by Brother Van in that church. He recounted that Charles Russell had been present that evening to hear his old friend preach. Dad worshiped Charlie Russell, whose paintings hung in some of the bars he sang in. That remark made Dad listen.

He didn't remember the sermon of course. What he remembered was Dad walking forward, bawling as if he were Irish, something Dad swore he'd never do, in public or private.

Of all the conversions he'd ever seen, Dad's was the most complete. He stopped drinking that night, never to start up again.

After a few tries with Methodist churches, they ended up Baptist. Dad learned sacred music and Baptist preaching. Then they were on the revival circuit. It was exciting. His dad was sweet to him. He never hit him or yelled at him once, ever again.

The quirk in the whole business was that now that Dad didn't drink when he played, he couldn't stand playing the pianos in the little old churches. He didn't mind the sticky keys or the broken pedals, but he could not bear that they were so out of tune.

So Dad took up piano tuning. He made his living at it. They even hired him at big churches and colleges. He solved his dilemma by bringing his tools with him on revival. Whenever he sang at a church, especially one he'd never been to before, he arrived in the morning and tuned the piano a half-step flat. At lunch he tuned it up to A440, sans tuning fork, of course. At 5:00 he touched up the persnickety strings. That was the only way he could play. The tuning was gratis. Well, actually, it was for him.

Dad sang and played and preached in churches for twenty-five years. Dad was real proud when his son became an educated, full-time preacher.

The Rich B—— from Helena

On Harbor Boulevard he saw the billboard advertising the hot-line ministry that local churches had set up. He'd spearheaded the effort. For the first time, he wished there had been a child-abuse hotline when he was a kid.

He'd never had *that* thought before. It felt hot and treasonous. He'd been involved in child-abuse issues as an adult because he cared. Since his dad had quit pounding on him, he figured his family was a success story and others could emulate the power of his dad's turnaround.

It came on him like an earthquake. His guts rumbled, and beads of sweat formed on his bald spot as he recalled beating up his own son over little things. He remembered wondering back then why his hand just kept coming down again and again on his baby's body while the child screamed and screamed. He remembered walking away feeling justified and ashamed. Depression would follow, for hours. He tried making up with the child later. Now his son was a successful businessman and active in a church. He wondered: maybe grace skips generations.

He switched channels to his dad's funeral, held in the Methodist church in Havre, the only church in town big enough to hold the service. The family flew from Santa Ana to Great Falls, where they rented a car and drove to Havre. His teenage children had never seen so much empty space; he assured them that there was a city at the end of the road. They teased him mercilessly about using the word *city* for Havre.

The service was fun. Dad was well loved. There was a lot music, of course, and a good sermon. The testimonies were moving. The attenders laughed hard about how the Baptist churches on the highline had the best-tuned pianos in the world.

At the big dinner he got edgy. He finished his food, rose from his chair and bent down to say to his wife, "I need some air."

"It's twenty degrees below zero outside," she said curtly.

"I'm *from* here, remember?" he said as he turned toward the door.

Without speaking to anyone else, he walked through the dining hall directly to the coat room. He grabbed the heavy coat and hat he'd borrowed for the trip and went out into the early-evening darkness.

He felt free and he felt like walking. A half-inch of fresh snow had fallen, and it swooshed out of the way of his shoes as they hit the sidewalk. He didn't need boots or galoshes. He knew his black wingtips would not get wet tonight. He had no idea how long he would walk. Instinctively he worked his way downtown to places he'd known.

It was quiet. Just like when he was a kid. Back then he'd leave his room at night, when his dad was sleeping drunk, and walk around town to get some air and clear his head. He felt like that child again. It was wonderful, really. The streets of this town were his home; they always had been, always would be, and especially on cold, snowy nights when so few were out.

The railroad yards and tall, fat grain elevators were still there, silent, shrouded in snow. The yard lights made the falling snow-flakes shimmer, and the elevators seemed dark and dangerous. Tracks ran this way and that. Having to step over them made you pay attention to where you were going, and they encouraged daydreaming. There were the ravens. They hung around the elevators for grain and mice and trash. He recalled shooting at them with a slingshot when he was a kid. No matter how hard you slung, the stones glanced off the bird and fell to the dirt. Sometimes the bird didn't even fly away. He laughed to himself. He'd become as tough as a raven, he thought.

Walking down Main Street he saw the shops he used to frequent and thought of the people who ran them, and how lucky he thought their kids were. He remembered how lucky he felt when the town looked up to his dad after his conversion. They never had much money, but everyone knew his dad was brilliant. When he was at Northern Montana College in Havre, music teachers would come up to him with remarks about his father's gifts.

The cold and the snow and the walking in the old neighborhood acted on him like a drug. I think the rhythm of the snowfall, his steps, his breathing and his heartbeat hypnotized him. He felt free to feel things. That was when he came upon the bar where his dad sang "Danny Boy" for the Irish travelers.

Clem's Howdy-Do had burned out some years earlier. The neon sign with the smiling man tipping his hat was gone, but from the window it looked as if the charred remains were pretty much in place. His mind became quiet and curious. He walked around back and found a door he could pry open. It felt illegal, which of course it was, but he knew he needed to go in for a little while.

The charred piano stood in the same place. The blackened tables sat where he'd remembered them. He thought of the mean old German who owned the place, standing behind the bar, glaring at Dad, wishing he could fire him. He couldn't; Dad was good for business. The man's wife was a peach. She fed him and kept him doing homework through those long, bad years.

Finding a chair spared from the blaze, he settled into the dark, and images began to run this way and that in his mind. One stood tall and dark and dangerous in back of the others. He'd never seen it before, and it was tough to focus on, but he worked at it. Slowly the other scenes subsided, and this one moved from the background to the foreground. Once he could see it clearly, the people in the picture began to move.

There was a young woman and a well-dressed man. The woman was looking at a small boy, about five years old. The well-dressed man clutched the woman's arm in one hand. With the other he held a gun on someone coming at him. He saw his father stomping and swerving and stumbling around tables and over chairs toward the well-dressed man, swinging a Civil War rifle he'd grabbed off the wall above the piano. The well-dressed man pulled the young woman out of the bar; though tense and afraid, she was not unwilling to leave.

When the bar door slammed, the scene was over. He sat shocked. The dream was not hard to figure out. He was the boy, the young woman was his mother, and now he finally knew who "the Rich Bastard from Helena" was.

The bar got all lit up with blinking blue and white lights coming from outside. A cop got out of his car and came up to the window. He called into the bar.

"Hey! Who's in there? Come out! Now!"

He picked himself up slowly and walked outside. He knew he wasn't really going to be in any trouble. Outside, the policeman looked him over and started lecturing him. "What are you doing in there? That's private property; you have no business in there."

He took it without saying anything. It didn't take long before the cop figured out that he was from out of town; but he didn't exactly look like a troublemaker.

"What were you doing in there anyway?" he inquired.

When he told him that he grew up in Havre and his dad used to play and sing in the bar, the officer offered to give him a ride to wherever he was staying. He politely declined.

On his way back to the funeral dinner, he faced a breeze and the cold air bit his skin, making him glad he lived in California.

Entering the warm moist air in the church, thick with talk, he stomped his feet on the rug inside the door.

Set Free

"Why did you just stomp your feet?" his wife inquired as they got out of the car.

"I don't know," he said, semihonestly.

He looked up at the old, stringy palm trees in front of the church and took a deep breath of thick, warm, smoggy air that insulted his lungs. But he smiled and he really felt good, better than he had in years. He walked to the church with the notes to the last sermon he would ever preach folded into his Bible, thinking of Jesus' words "The truth shall set you free." What a final sermon that would be! For a minute he was tempted to do what Dad would have done. Dad would have preached off the cuff. No, the sermon he prepared was good, and if he cut loose there was no telling what he would say. For the sake of his wife and the people in the church he dearly loved, he decided to preach from his notes.

During the service he felt lighter; the anger was gone. Truth, denied his soul for forty years, soothed and healed. He felt the satisfaction that comes from the completion of a gigantic task. His soul had sleuthed his brain for years. Now missing pieces of past events began fitting into place. Decades of his life returned to him. His soul's demand for truth gave way to the relief that fresh-won integrity provides.

At the meeting following the service, cradling a small sheet of white paper in his hand, he pressed the point of the little golf-pencil into the paper and it broke through, digging into his palm as he marked: "Dismiss." He could hardly believe that he had, for the first time, voted against himself, but he really felt good about it.

A space of peace formed in his soul. He felt emptier than in years and happier than he could remember. As his eyes fixed on the cross in the front of the sanctuary, he began to hear his father sing "Danny Boy" loud and clear, hitting every note so sweet and so high that you just knew his vocal cords came straight from heaven.

Slowly his face sank toward his knees. Mucus dripped out of his nose and mouth on to his pant legs. His wife's warm, strong arm reached across his shoulders and pulled him to her. He shook involuntarily in her lap.

Some people gathered around him while others left silently out the back. He felt fingers on his back and heard prayers on his behalf. For the first time in his life he felt God within him. *This is what Dad had*, he thought. Seizing the moment, he forgave the Rich Bastard from Helena, the woman who went away, and the young drunk who at least had kept him.

Eight

Holiness

Huckleberry Muffins

• •

*Only in this way, only when one is drawn into God's love can one become
certain of God. Certainty of God is not a normal
characteristic of the human consciousness, but is rather the event of
the renewal of all human relationships, including the
consciousness, through the fire of the love of God with which God desires
to grasp us and in which every person is totally
grasped by God. For that to happen, the* human word is needed
*which allows the triune God to be expressed in language
in that it tells the story of Jesus Christ as God's history with all people.*
Eberhard Jüngel, God as the Mystery of the World

I walk in a few minutes late as usual, but they hardly mind;
my lateness is their chat time. Three long, rectangular folding
tables pushed together in the middle of the Sunshine Room make
room for about fifteen. We call it the Sunshine Room because of
its many windows. It is half of a fellowship hall. When the church
built it in the 1970s, they could afford only half a building—and
barely that—so they erected a building with a vaulted ceiling that
ends at the peak. The wall on the tall half of the room is all
windows. What light!

Lucy has brought fresh huckleberry muffins. She passes them,
insisting that we take. Rhonda pours coffee.

"OK, ladies, let's get started." Turning to the Psalms, I find a
call to the study of the Word of God and read it:

There is a river whose streams make glad the city of God,

the holy habitation of the Most High.
God is in the midst of the city; it shall not be moved;
God will help it when the morning dawns. (Ps 46:4-5)
I pray.

"Lord, bless us with your presence this morning as we open your Word. Your Word is a river from your throne to our souls. It flows beside us this morning as we gather as friends in Christ. Help us to dip our cups into that river and drink deeply of the Word of God; in Jesus' name, amen."

As I lift my head I see Lucy. Lucy, her husband and their four young children moved here from Iowa. They left a rat's nest of family problems and high-paying jobs. After eighteen months the beauty of the land has not healed them; rather, it has darn near starved them. How right the Montana lady was who lived in a deserted dancehall for sixty years: "You can't eat the scenery—'course that don't keep people from trying." On the other hand, I admire Lucy and her family for having the guts to come here and take a shot at a new life. They might just make it.

Chapter Five

"Well, let's see, I think we're on Revelation 5 this week. Let's listen to Alexander Scourby." I snap the play button on the boom box.

With a voice as rich as prairie topsoil, Scourby intones: "Chapter five . . ." Click. I stop the machine.

"Wouldn't you love to be able to say 'chapter five' like that? Listen to him again." They chuckle with me. I rewind the tape.

"Chapter five." I rewind it. Snap.

"Chapter five." Rewind. Snap.

"Chapter five." Rewind. Snap.

We're laughing by now, and it is all a joke, but it is more than just a joke. I'm forcing them to listen to sounds. Words are sounds as much as they are symbols. In Revelation we generally become so engrossed in the symbols that we fail to let the sounds of the words conjure the pictures in our minds that sanctify our imaginations. We will talk about the symbols. But first the sounds must establish a beachhead in our souls.

Snap. We settle in to listen. As the reading begins, some look down, some look up, some stare forward. We focus on something far, far away, very deep inside. Our cognitive guard is down. The grids and filters of defense and repression are set aside. We do not fear hearing the Word of God. Dead still, we listen in soul-yielding obedience.

And I saw in the right hand of him that sat on the throne a book written within and on the backside, sealed with seven seals.

And I saw a strong angel proclaiming with a loud voice, Who is worthy to open the book, and to loose the seals thereof?

And no man in heaven, nor in earth, neither under the earth, was able to open the book, neither to look thereon. And I wept much, because no man was found worthy to open and to read the book, neither to look thereon.

And one of the elders saith unto me, Weep not: behold, the Lion of the tribe of Juda, the Root of David, hath prevailed to open the book, and to loose the seven seals thereof.

And I beheld, and, lo, in the midst of the throne and of the four beasts, and in the midst of the elders, stood a Lamb as it had been slain, having seven horns and seven eyes, which are the seven Spirits of God sent forth into all the earth.

And he came and took the book out of the right hand of him that sat upon the throne.

And when he had taken the book, the four beasts and four and twenty elders fell down before the Lamb, having every one of them harps, and golden vials full of odours, which are the prayers of saints.

And they sung a new song, saying, Thou art worthy to take the book, and to open the seals thereof: for thou wast slain, and hast redeemed us to God by thy blood out of every kindred, and tongue, and people, and nation;

And hast made us unto our God kings and priests: and we shall reign on the earth.

And I beheld, and I heard the voice of many angels round about the throne and the beasts and the elders: and the number of them was ten thousand times ten thousand, and thousands of thousands;

Saying with a loud voice, Worthy is the Lamb that was slain to receive power, and riches, and wisdom, and strength, and honour, and glory, and blessing.

And every creature which is in heaven, and on the earth, and under the earth, and such as are in the sea, and all that are in them, heard I saying, Blessing, and honour, and glory, and power, be unto him that sitteth upon the throne, and unto the Lamb for ever and ever.

And the four beasts said, Amen. And the four and twenty elders fell down and worshipped him that liveth for ever and ever. (Rev 5 KJV)

The Mystery of the Scroll

LILLY: What poetry!

PASTOR: Exactly!

Lilly's a great lady. She and her husband converted ten years ago, in their late sixties. She brings little or no theological prejudice to the text; that is a big advantage when reading Revelation. She listens to the beauty of language, with an ever-new joy that God uses human language to communicate himself to us.

She continues.

LILLY: It's a great drama. The stage is heaven. The images flow in and out in different scenes. I like this!

MOLLY   *(Interrupting—an acceptable practice in our group)* What is the scroll and what are the seals?

PASTOR: The scroll is the will of God. The scroll is the mystery of the plan of God, the providence of God worked out in the history of the world. The mystery of all of our lives are contained in the scroll. The seals are the things that must take place in the process of the unfolding of the plan of God. These things that must take place are happening all the time, although they will happen with greater intensity at the end of time.

Layla, a woman about fifty years old, perks up. Success consistently eludes Layla. She's terribly able, but can't do the final thing in any task that will bring her satisfaction. She is talented and well educated, but jobs never work out. Her kids, all grown, love her and hate her. None of her three former husbands can bring themselves to dislike her, or to live with her. Layla is great to have in a Bible study because she sees things honestly, personally and differently.

Lion and Lamb

LAYLA: What I like about this story is the way that the Lion becomes the Lamb. I think it is ironic that the conquering hero of the story is the Lamb that has been slaughtered.

PASTOR: That's right, keep going.

LAYLA: That's all I have to say. *(She smiles broadly and looks away just a little.)*

PASTOR: Let's reread the text here.

"Then one of the elders said to me, 'Do not weep. See, the Lion of the tribe of Judah, the Root of David, has conquered, so that he can open the scroll and its seven seals.' Then I saw between the throne and the four living creatures and among the elders a Lamb standing as if it had been slaughtered, having seven horns and seven eyes, which are the seven spirits of God sent out into all the earth."

Rhonda, about thirty-five and the kindest woman now living on planet earth, jumps in, *assertively.*

RHONDA: The Lord wins the battle with Christ's death. Only the Lamb can open the seals.

Layla jams an observation into the mix.

LAYLA: On our ranch growing up, the sheep were the stupidest animals. The chickens s sowed more sense than the sheep.

LUCY: You never had turkeys!

LAYLA: Father hated turkeys. He wouldn't have them on
              the ranch.
PASTOR: Back to the text, ladies!
LAYLA: *(Somewhat scoldingly)* I think this does pertain to
              the meaning of the text. It is pertinent that sheep
              are stupid . . .

As she rambles on I wonder if St. John thought the stupidity of
sheep was part of the point. This strikes me as doubtful. Certainly
St. John knew that sheep are dumb; I'm just not sure the cognitive
capacities of sheep were on his mind here. But Layla is famous for
quirky connections that somehow work. So I listen carefully, real-
izing that the Spirit may well be speaking through her.

LAYLA: After all, what does the Lamb do? The Lamb is
              slaughtered. Just like real lambs. It takes no skill
              to do what the Lamb does. The Lamb isn't neces-
              sarily good at anything. The Lamb just dies . . .

My turn to interrupt.

PASTOR: Layla, I think you may have a really good point
              here. Let's look at Romans 8. You've hit on some-
              thing; let's look at your idea in another place in
              the Bible.

I read the text.

Who will separate us from the love of Christ? Will hardship,
or distress, or persecution, or famine, or nakedness, or peril,
or sword? As it is written,

"For your sake we are being killed all day long;
    we are accounted as sheep to be slaughtered."

No, in all these things we are more than conquerors through
him who loved us. For I am convinced that neither death, nor
life, nor angels, nor rulers, nor things present, nor things to
come, nor powers, nor height, nor depth, nor anything else in
all creation, will be able to separate us from the love of God in
Christ Jesus our Lord. (Rom 8:35-39)

Lambs and the Lamb

LILLY: Does this mean that we are the Lamb?

PASTOR: No—not exactly. No, the Lamb in Revelation 5 does something special that only he can do. Only his blood is the redeeming blood; he is the unique Savior. After all, only he can open the seals, and only he is the Lion of Judah and the Root of David. We are not that, but still, for all of our differences from him, we share something very special and very important with the Lamb. We, like he, are lined up to be slain, and his death is so powerful in its redemption that no power of evil in the whole universe can separate us from that redeeming love. Somehow we are like him, and there is a connection between the way God opens the seal and saves the world by the Lamb that is slain and the way we participate in that as his followers. It has to do, at the very least, with the fact that just as Jesus saves the world and conquers the powers through his sacrifice, we are like that in our work. Just as Jesus could not, we cannot use violence to accomplish God's work.

Here's another way to look at it; turn to Isaiah 53.

I wait for them to find it, and I read selections.

Surely he has borne our infirmities
    and carried our diseases;
yet we accounted him stricken,
    struck down by God, and afflicted.
But he was wounded for our transgressions,
    crushed for our iniquities;
upon him was the punishment that made us whole,
    and by his bruises we are healed.
All we like sheep have gone astray;
    we have all turned to our own way,
and the LORD has laid on him
    the iniquity of us all.
He was oppressed, and he was afflicted,

yet he did not open his mouth;
like a lamb that is led to the slaughter,
and like a sheep that before its shearers is silent,
so he did not open his mouth. (vv. 4-7)

PASTOR: Now we know that this prophecy is about Jesus.
There is no question about the fact that what
Isaiah is prophesying here is fulfilled in the life of
Jesus, in the unfolding of the whole plan of God
for the redemption of the world. But scholars
struggle with this text because they know that just
as much as it means an individual, it also means a
group. This prophecy is not only about Jesus, it
is about the destiny and role of the whole people
of God.

They look confused. I am too. But I feel as if we're making
headway into something important, so, not knowing where we
are going, I pursue our similarity to the Lamb of God slain.

PASTOR: Turn to Mark 8; I'm not sure what verse it is, we'll
find it when we get there . . . here it is, verses 31
through 34:
"Then he began to teach them that the Son of
Man must undergo great suffering, and be rejected by the elders, the chief priests, and the
scribes, and be killed, and after three days rise
again. He said all this quite openly. And Peter
took him aside and began to rebuke him. But
turning and looking at his disciples, he rebuked
Peter and said, 'Get behind me, Satan! For you
are setting your mind not on divine things but on
human things.'
"He called the crowd with his disciples, and said
to them, 'If any want to become my followers, let
them deny themselves and take up their cross
and follow me.' "

Jesus tells us that we must pick up *our cross* and
follow him. Christ is the suffering servant in

Isaiah 53, but we are included in that too. So you see, in the Gospel story Jesus includes us with him in the role of the suffering servant.

Now what does Peter do?

LILLY: Peter scolds Jesus for suggesting that he must be killed.

PASTOR: Why does he do that?

RHONDA: Because they expected the Messiah to come with military power and defeat the Romans?

PASTOR: Yes, to some extent, but there is something more here. The issue revolves around what one's proper relationship to a Messiah is. Your comment, Rhonda, was correct. What needs to be added is that the disciples expected to follow Jesus and participate with him in the great victory. You see, a Messiah must be followed. You can listen to a teacher, watch a martyr, obey a prophet, but you must follow a Messiah. This is why Peter is so exasperated with Jesus for suggesting that the Son of Man must suffer and die. Peter knows that he in some way will be called into suffering with Jesus. Jesus in turn responds to Peter with the most stinging rebuke he delivered to anyone: "Get behind me, Satan!" He delivers this blow because he knows that what Peter is speaking against is the essence of Christian discipleship, and that in this situation Peter really is speaking on behalf of the devil.

Think about it: throughout the Gospels the devil only tempts Jesus not to go to the cross. In the same way, the devil prompts us in our lives to put down the cross of discipleship. Jesus defeated the devil on the cross, and the devil is defeated as we carry our cross. This brings us back to Revelation, doesn't it? This is why the Lamb that was slain is the Lion of the tribe of Judah, the King of David.

The book of Revelation has a reputation for containing much violence and bloodshed. In one respect it deserves its reputation. However, it is infrequently noted that the victory is won in the death of Christ. *We* never lift a finger in violence against anyone. The book of Revelation may contain the best argument for pacifism in the Bible.

By the way—why does John weep?

LAYLA: He is weeping because he feels helpless against the mystery of the will of God and the problem of evil in the world. I've felt that way many times. Many nights I've sat alone in my front room and wept because I felt helpless in the face of the challenges of my life. But it seems like the Lord comes and comforts me, and I continue on.

It's been like that in my life. I come to the end of my rope, and just when I am beside myself, the Lord comes and sits beside me and hugs me, and I feel like someone is with me that loves me very much. I feel it in my soul. No matter what my problems are, I know that he is with me and will protect me.

She's struck a chord with all of us. God has been with us too.

The Devil Defeated

PASTOR: What do you think, Layla: when Jesus has been with you over the years, in those really tough times, would you say that it has been Jesus, the Lion of the tribe of Judah, the conquering King, or the Lamb of God?

LAYLA: Both. He is my conquering King, but he also comes to me as the Lamb of God. When I am alone and feel terrible and unlovable, he comes to me as the Lamb of God.

PASTOR: So the devil has been defeated in your life by the Lamb of God too.

LAYLA: Yes, I think so. I think Jesus has come to me many times as the Lamb of God. I think that is why he comforts me. He can comfort me because he has suffered pain and rejection too.

PASTOR: How about the rest of you? Can any of you identify with this? Have you had times when you were very low and Jesus came and comforted you?

LUCY: I hope I can say this here—well, I guess I'll just say it . . . I was raped when I was a teenager . . .

Lucy's eyes are unable to meet ours, so she looks down at the table, her eyes fix on the muffins, but she is seeing something deep inside her. She hesitates over it, but you can tell she wants to keep talking, so we stay quiet while she gathers energy and figures out how to word it.

LUCY: After that I used to be awake at night a lot, crying and crying and wondering how God could have let this happen. Pastor, why does God let things like that happen?

PASTOR: I don't know why things like that happen . . .

For a moment I think about the unbelievable amount of child abuse that has been going on out in the middle-of-nowhere ranches in Montana for generations. These ladies will understand. So I simply say, "Why don't you just keep telling us your story?"

LUCY: I was so mad at God. I was mad at myself and just plain mad at everyone and everything. And I was ashamed, really ashamed. But just like Layla said, there were those times when I felt that God was with me, really close. All around me and inside me, and my body and my soul felt warm and secure. Then I could go to sleep. That was the Lamb of God. That was the Lamb of God . . .

Layla places her arm around Lucy.

LUCY: I felt so dirty, so sinful, so unacceptable to God. I felt like I must have deserved what happened to me—but when Jesus came and comforted me, for that little time I felt clean and whole and all right. That was the Lamb of God.

LAYLA: That was the Lamb of God defeating the devil.

RHONDA: The Lamb of God does not condemn us or accuse us.

LUCY: I guess I see that now. It's been hard, but God has brought me through it. I'm so grateful for my wonderful husband and our wonderful little children ... For a long time I wanted to kill the man who did it to me. But it just ate me up inside. I'm not sure I have forgiven him, or that I ever can forgive him. But I do know that God will deal with him in his way at his time. I know God will deal with him.

LAYLA: He is the Lion of the tribe of Judah, sweetheart; he is the judge. We can trust God to judge that man. You can let go of that because God is that man's judge; you don't need to be.

Lucy just nods. But the group isn't paying that much attention to her anymore. Everything is silent, and as I glance around the table, the women, each of them, are looking down, thinking of something themselves. One breaks open a muffin, another sips coffee, and Lucy smiles through wet eyes as Layla continues to hold her. There is little question in my mind that Layla understands precisely what Lucy is going through.

Part 3

The Soul Redeemed

....

Nine

War Against God

∙∙∙

*R*ivers possess metaphysical characteristics that run deeper than symbolism. Of course every river does carry symbolic value. Around here the Yellowstone River symbolizes the wild river; it is the longest undammed river in the lower forty-eight United States. However, it symbolizes a wild river only to some. To others the Yellowstone symbolizes an untapped resource, a river begging for dams and mining operations. The rivers of the Columbia River Basin at one time symbolized salmon. Then they symbolized cheap electricity and irrigation water. Now they symbolize the tradeoff of one resource for another.

Sometimes it goes the other way. The Clark Fork of the Columbia River in western Montana was, in the first half of the twentieth century, a sewer for heavy metals from the copper mines and smelters of Butte and Anaconda, and for hog carcasses from slaughterhouses in Missoula. Its drainage represents the largest federal Superfund environmental cleanup project in the

United States. No one alive today remembers an unpolluted Clark Fork. But with a modicum of care over the last few decades, the Clark Fork is now a fine-looking river—alive, productive, filled with trout, and an economic and spiritual asset to the communities through which it winds its quiet way.

Rivers symbolize pain. The Little Big Horn River and the Big Hole River flowed past battles between Native and European Americans.

If a river's value is merely symbolic, we have little control over its fate. Contradictory symbols compete for the imagination. Too often money wins the battle, because symbols can be manipulated in the public mind with advertising campaigns. If and when we stop caring that the Yellowstone River is our longest undammed river, surely it will yield to concrete, steel and turbines. All to bring wealth to people who do not live on its banks, who hire small planes to fly them beyond roads to the undammed rivers, beyond the ken of normal people.

The Site of Battle

Ever so much deeper, unpolluted rivers possess metaphysical characteristics. They are densely populated with delicate life forms woven together in intricate, symbiotic existence. Rivers are shot through with soul, the very stuff of life. Insofar as all living creatures are *nephesh chayyah*, living souls filled with the breath of life, rivers flow with soul.

It is more than poetry to talk of the soul of a river, though it is unashamedly poetic; and we refuse to imagine a world in which the souls of rivers no longer inspire the souls of poets and painters.

The line between the plants and animals of a river and its inanimate physical characteristics—the minerals dissolved in it, for instance—is as permeable as a cell membrane. Every aspect of a river contributes to its life. Furthermore, a river's environment does not stop at its banks. A river's ecosystem spreads over its banks to include the entire watershed above and below the surface of the ground. A river supports abundant life in its surrounding countryside, including birds, large and small mammals, reptiles, insects and the most wonderful and the most troublesome animal on its banks, humans. We can enjoy and make a profit from the bounties of a great river without destroying its life. The only requirement is that we care for its spiritual and physical nature.

Most of us recognize the tragedy of pouring chemicals into a river. Yet the greatest pollutant of Montana rivers is silt. Silt is natural and is in all rivers. But when mining, logging, ranching and road-building operations indiscriminately scar a river's drainage, stream runoff hauls cut-loose silt into the river. This silt fills in the spaces between the hand-sized rocks and pea gravel in the river. What's so bad about that?

Most of the life of a river lives on and around its rocks and gravel. Water flows around the rocks, providing oxygen and nutrients to the microorganisms that live on them. We experience these tiny *nephesh chayyah* as slime. In a Montana river, the soul is in the slime. Slimy rocks are aqueous hay fields where insects feed during larval stages. These insects in turn feed the trout, which in turn feed the birds of prey and mammals on the shores of the river as well as humans. The pea-gravel beds of a river are where the trout lay their eggs. The eggs survive in the pea gravel protected and oxygenated by moving water until the minnows hatch. When silt fills the space between rocks previously immersed in free-flowing, nutrient- and oxygen-rich water, the river suffocates.

It is not poetic, symbolic or sentimental: destroying a river is war against God. Poisoning a river, completely dewatering a river (including its feeder streams) or silting a river destroys the work of God's Spirit breathing the breath of life into the animal life of the river. It isn't wrong to catch, kill and eat fish, or to use river water to irrigate crops. The problem is not the killing of any particular animal in a river. It isn't wrong to fish or hunt, or even to shoot gophers. What's wrong is the destruction of an entire interdependent web of life so that it cannot rejuvenate itself. It is war against the Spirit of God and the plan of God within that river.

If God created the world and superintends the world, whole rivers and the life they support are part of his gracious plan. To cripple the life web of a river is to devalue the plan of God and to asphyxiate the work of the Spirit of God in the river's life.

It's all a piece of the same thing. The destruction of rivers, land, animals and humans is war against God. Man's inhumanity to man is only one aspect of man's inhumanity to all of creation and man's inhumanity to God.

The environmental crisis is a part of the larger problem of evil. Not just because the destruction of the natural world is evil, but because the destruction of the natural world is doubling back on us and promises large-scale human destruction.

Is Dualism the Problem?

Some blame Christianity for the environmental crisis. They blame it for what appears to be an attitude of dominance over creation instead of cooperation with creation. But blaming Christianity for the environmental crisis ignores the fact that the worst environmental disasters of the past century occurred in communist countries and are occurring in areas of Asia and Africa that are not overtly Christian. It also ignores the fact that the environmental movement began in nations with a strong Christian heritage.

Yet there is another complaint we must deal with. This one needs to be taken seriously: the complaint that the cause of the environmental crisis is not Christianity but the Christian dualism of matter and spirit, body and soul. We cannot ignore this issue, because in this study I am professing a very real, if minimal, dualism.

Christians debate this issue hotly. For the past few decades, it must be said, those decrying dualism have seemed to be firmly in control of the debate. Dualism, the good ol' boy of Western civilization, is being blamed for the destruction of the earth.

There is a certain logic to this. Some elements of the argument cannot be denied. Ultimately, however, the argument fails because there are many forms of dualism, some of which are bad and some of which are good. Lumping all forms of dualism together isn't fair and isn't good thinking. It isn't historically or spiritually accurate. Take the fact that Native American culture is profoundly dualistic, as are Amish and Hutterite cultures. No one blames those cultures for environmental destruction.

The best way to examine the argument that dualism is the cause of the environmental crisis is to study its best representative. What we find is that the gentleman all hot and bothered about Christian dualism is himself a deep-seated dualist. His argument is good to the extent that he isolates dualism in its worst form, but he doesn't give it the right historical name. He demonizes dualism where to be more accurate he should isolate a pervasive dualist virus, gnosticism.

Creation Formed by Love

Wendell Berry is a Kentucky dirt farmer, poet, novelist, essayist and sometime professor of English who writes passionately about human community and careful farming. My introduction to Berry came from Eugene Peterson, who told me that Berry was his best mentor in pastoral ministry. Eugene told me, "Wendell Berry has poured his whole life into making the soil on one farm better. When I read him on farming, whenever he says 'farm' or 'soil,' I insert 'church' or 'parish.' It works every time. Wendell Berry taught me to care for a parish like he cares for his farm."

I started pastoring that way, and it works for me too. Reading Berry is a treat. He crafts words the way he farms, carefully, with strong hands. Sometimes he writes as if he's pounding in a fencepost; at other times he's planting a seedling. Occasionally you get the sense he is shoveling out the barn.

Whereas Wendell Berry defends the Christian faith vigorously in the face of naysayers who impugn it for the environmental crisis,[1] he is death on Christian dualism. I think he goes too far.

To Berry's way of thinking, dualism, the idea that matter and spirit are in some way separate realities, has allowed us to degrade matter in favor of what we consider "spiritual." This, he believes, gives us license to use anything we consider mere matter any way we want, for our own profit, regardless of the consequences. As he says: "If you are going to destroy creatures without respect, you will want to reduce them to 'materiality'; you will want to deny that there is spirit or truth in them, just as you will want to believe that the only holy creatures, the only creatures with souls, are humans—or even only Christian humans."[2] Elsewhere he says, "What I'm arguing against here is not complexity or mystery but dualism. . . . This dualism inevitably reduces physical reality, and it does so by removing its mystery from it, by dividing it absolutely from what dualist thinkers have understood as spiritual or mental reality."[3]

Berry becomes more specific about his distaste for dualism when he says,

I have been talking of course about a dualism that manifests itself in several ways: as a cleavage, a radical discontinuity, between Creator and creature, spirit and matter, religion and nature, religion and economy, worship and work, and so on. This dualism I think is the most destructive disease that afflicts us. In its best known, its most dangerous and perhaps fundamental version, it is the dualism of body and soul. . . .

And the secular version of the same dualism has been that the body, along with the rest of the "material" world, must give way before the advance of the human mind. The dominant religious view, for a long time, has been that the body is a kind of scrip issued by the Great Company Store in the Sky, which can be cashed in to redeem the soul but is otherwise worthless. And the predictable result has been a human creature able to appreciate or tolerate only the "spiritual" (or mental) part of the Creation and full of semi-conscious hatred of the "physical" or "natural" part, which is ready and willing to destroy for "salvation," for profit, for "victory," or for fun. This madness constitutes the norm for modern humanity and of modern Christianity.[4]

In his defense, Berry's world is exquisite and spiritual. "I believe that Creation is one continuous fabric comprehending simultaneously what we mean by 'spirit' and what we mean by 'matter.' "[5]

He admits the existence of the soul; he just doesn't think we should speculate about any differences between the body and the soul. "I do not doubt the reality of the experience and knowledge we call 'spiritual' any more than I doubt the reality of the so-called physical experience and knowledge: I recognize the rough utility of these terms. But I strongly doubt the advantage, and even the possibility, of separating these two realities."[6] He recognizes the reality of spirit and dust in creation. "Our bodies live, the Bible says, by the spirit and breath of God, but it does not say how this is so. We are not going to *know* about this."[7]

The fact is, Wendell Berry is a dualist. Statements like the following are dualistic in nature:

I take literally the statement in the Gospel of John that God loves the world. I believe that the world was created and approved by love, that it subsists, coheres, and endures by love, and that, insofar as it is redeemable, it can be redeemed only by love. I believe that divine love, incarnate and indwelling in the world, summons the world always toward wholeness, which ultimately is reconciliation and atonement with God.[8]

Farmer Berry is a man pickled in spirit.

Wendell Berry's deep dualism is the source of his strength. Though he is a poet, his metaphysical understanding of the land he works goes deeper than mere symbolism. He is not a hardpan empiricist with an antiquarian cultural interest in spirit. He cares for the land because it is alive, it has been alive, and under his stewardship its life increases. With intelligent sweat his spirit can make the land better: he can work in its life as part of its life. His personal experience of the spiritual reality inhering in all existence is the source of his love for land, all living things and the ecological community of all life. It is the source of his prophecy on behalf of the preservation and care of all creation. (You see, I really do like this guy a lot.)

However, by denigrating dualism as a cliché for what he doesn't like, he does his own cause a disservice. He himself says in yet another essay, "When history has been reduced to cliché, we need to return to the study of history."[9]

Gnosticism and the Devaluation of Matter

Wendell Berry's enemy—and our enemy—is not dualism, it is gnosticism. He reveals this understanding in an essay in which he defines further what he means by the term *dualism:* "if we think of ourselves as lofty souls trapped temporarily in lowly bodies in a dispirited, desperate, unlovable world that we must despise for Heaven's sake . . ."[10] This is classic gnosticism.

Gnosticism is a name given to a diverse religious movement active in and around the church in the early centuries of its existence. The religious movement itself died out over a thousand years ago, but gnostic beliefs have proved exceedingly durable and are prevalent in the modern world.

Gnostic belief is dualist, but it is a dualism of a different order from the dualism of the Judeo-Christian tradition, or even Persian, Platonic or Indian dualism. Kurt Rudolph tells us,

> The Gnostic dualism is distinguished from those above all in the one essential point, that it is "anti-cosmic"; that is, its [gnosticism's] conception includes an unequivocally negative evaluation of the visible world together with its creator; it ranks as a kingdom of evil and darkness. The identification of "evil" and "matter," which is not found in Iranian and Zoroastrian thought, occurs in Gnosis as a fundamental conception.[11]

Gnosticism is a religion of redemption by means of knowledge.[12] J. N. D. Kelly describes this characteristic for us: "In all the Gnostic systems redemption is brought about by knowledge, and it is the function of the divine mediators to open the eyes of 'pneumatic' men to the truth."[13] Kelly goes on to say, "In other words, when a man has really grasped the Gnostic myths in all their inwardness, and thus realizes who he is, how he has come to his present condition, and what is the 'indescribable Greatness' which is the supreme God, the spiritual element in him begins to free itself from the entanglements of matter."[14]

A curious characteristic of many gnostics interests me a great deal. It is the ironic twist that since the early gnostics degraded matter, they tended to use it and abuse it wantonly as something that had no substantial value. Sexual and material excess was not uncommon. The gnostic figured that the world was evil and matter didn't matter. As long as one believed the truth, why not use and abuse the world at will?

That is the belief system Berry despises, and which we must also despise. It is the identification of "evil" and "matter" that offends Wendell Berry, and it should offend us. Matter is not something that entangles us; it is our blessed existence.

From the Inside Out

We part ways with gnosticism absolutely. Whereas gnosticism teaches that evil comes to us from the outside in—from the outward, evil, material world—the Scriptures teach that spiritual evil comes from the inside out. As Jesus says:

> "Do you not see that whatever goes into a person from outside cannot defile, since it enters, not the heart but the stomach, and goes out into the sewer?" (Thus he declared all foods clean.) And he said, "It is what comes out of a person that defiles. For it is from within, from the human heart, that evil intentions come: fornication, theft, murder, adultery, avarice, wickedness, deceit, licentiousness, envy, slander, pride, folly. All these evil things come from within, and they defile a person." (Mk 7:18-23)

Of course you don't have to know that you have a soul, or how it works, or how your body and your soul interact, to function wonderfully as a whole person—except for the fact of sin. The problem of sin forces us to consider the human soul. It forces us to ask where sin comes from, and where and how sin in us is solved and cured by God. If we do not take seriously the spiritual soul and its role in sin, we have no choice, ironically, but to blame the body.

We cannot blame the body for sin. A rapist is not a man with a bad penis. When a woman is raped, or a child is raped, or a community is raped, or a race is raped, or a nation is raped, or the land and its rivers are raped, it is the work of spiritual evil. It is the work of the human heart at war against God. This is precisely what gnosticism denies.

Acknowledging human existence in body and soul, far from causing us to denigrate the body or matter, allows us to see evil for what it is. Evil is spiritual in nature. That helps us locate the place of cure.

You don't need to know that you have a liver until it doesn't work anymore. Then you need to know as much about it as possible. Farmer Berry, I assume, prefers to see his soil as an organic whole, but when his crops stop growing right, he needs to know the soil's makeup. He will analyze it and add what is missing.

The Holy Spirit breathes the human soul into existence: how can it be evil? We cannot say that the human soul is evil. Nor can we say that a sinful soul is a soul filled with an evil spirit.

Yet we do have evil in our spirit. To use the metaphor of the sponge, our soul does live in an environment of sin, and it breathes and exhales pollutants. But that is not saying enough. It is too much to say that the human soul is evil, but it is not enough to say that only the human spirit is evil but not the soul. Somehow, human evil has its origins in the human soul.

Rage Against God

Sin's origins are not in the soul itself, but the potential for sin originates in the soul's emptiness. The soul's utter vulnerability over and against itself, its utter dependence on God the Holy Spirit's continual breathing, is the *location* of human sin. We possess our existence in risk.

Sin is the refusal to exercise faith in the veracity of God to keep soul and body alive. Our dependence is not bad. Animal souls are dependent on the Holy Spirit, and they are not sinful. It is the divinity in humankind, as John Calvin himself termed it, that creates the crisis. Sin's deepest origins lie in our greatest similarities with God. We are at war against God not in our dissimilarity with God but at the point of our greatest similarity.

In the magisterial name "I AM THAT I AM" God states his unconditioned existence. In our analogous "I am" we state our radically conditioned, vulnerable existence, made for fellowship and covenant with God and with one another. Yet we refuse to be satisfied with the difference in our names. We cannot be satisfied with life lived in analogy to God; we feel we must live as God. We assert our existence over and against God in rebellion against him. We fill our empty souls, made to be cathedrals, with false divinity—idols—with dreams and schemes and denial.

And yet only something as radically good as a human being, a being as close to God as any creature can ever be, could ever be as evil we are. This is why all sin is sin against God. As David said in his classic confession of sin:

Against you, you alone, have I sinned,
and done what is evil in your sight,
so that you are justified in your sentence
and blameless when you pass judgment. (Ps 51:4)

Accordingly, all sin is also sin against self. Not just against the body, but against the image of God. This rage against God, the image of God, the plan of God, the creation of God—in the case of the destruction of a river—comes from something in us from birth. As David goes on to say,

Indeed, I was born guilty,
a sinner when my mother conceived me. (v. 5)

Perhaps the origin of the disease may be seen in what David says next:

You desire truth in the inward being;
therefore teach me wisdom in my secret heart. (v. 6)

The true heart believes God. To believe God is to cast our life into his life as our true origin and destiny. The believing heart knows God's love as his active presence.

Unbelief believes in God but resents God; it cannot believe God wills good for it. It is the lie of unbelief that taints our soul throughout, and no matter how much good we manage to accomplish in our lives, unbelief causes us ever and again to deal with God, self, fellow humans and creation faithlessly.

The Soul Must Be Saved

We need salvation consistent with God's desire to save humanity and creation, which gives the lie to our unbelief and which solves our guilt over his destroyed creation and his offended holiness. We need new hearts created by God.

The soul must be saved and it must be healed. When we say that the soul must be saved, we are not proposing that the soul be saved and the body be damned. The soul must be saved because it is the soul that is lost, it is the soul that bears the guilt, it is the soul that is unbelieving, and it is the soul that goes to hell.

It is too easy to say glibly that we need to save the body as well as the soul. What does that mean? Does that mean the body is sinful? Does it mean the body is defective? Will a low-cholesterol diet and good exercise save the body from sin and guilt? Praying for daily bread and taking care of our bodies are good, but when it comes to guilt and evil, the body does not need to be saved—because it is not evil. The soul must be saved because the soul is depraved and guilty.

What about the flesh? Do not the Scriptures suggest that the flesh is evil? What about world? Do not the Scriptures suggest that the world is evil? The words *world, flesh* and *body* are used in Scripture to describe good things. They did take on negative theological meaning in some sections of the New Testament. *World, flesh* and *body* in some passages mean the system of sin in the world and in us. They represent our physical and spiritual insatiability from inside out. The body is involved in sin through the rebellion coming from the core of our being. Body and soul make us whole people, and we do indeed sin as whole persons!

Ten

Overreligion

••

A little religion goes a *lawng* way," an old dying cowboy told
me. He looked me square in the eyeballs to see if he'd managed
to rankle me. I didn't blink.

In fact, I laughed and said, "I agree completely." Then I got
straight-faced, looked *him* square in the eyeballs and said, "I know
the truth of that better than you do. Believe me, Phil, nobody gets
their belly full of religion worse than a preacher does."

He gave me a "yup" and a cowboy nod, telling me that he
respected my point. A preacher doesn't get that kind of compliment too often from guys like this, so I felt pretty good.

His wife Susan sighed and smiled nervously. Phil didn't like
preachers. He thought they were stuffy and greedy, something I
wasn't able to dispute. He'd been hassling them for years.

Susan grew up in our church. Though she had not attended
regularly for over fifty years, she sent offerings several times a
year. Naturally that brought the ministers out calling. Phil didn't

have a problem with Susan's sending offerings. But he suspected visiting ministers of wanting more money—or even worse, wanting him to come to church. His opinions about ministers didn't make him a minority in the cowboy crowd. Still, I think he liked talking about not liking preachers more than he really didn't like them. It was just common talk, like arguing over the weather or cussin' change.

He hadn't figured out how to get under my skin yet. Susan couldn't believe it. He even looked forward to my visits. Phil was motivated. He was sick and crippled up. We knew there wasn't much time left. His best buddy had died recently of a heart attack. Another one of his old-time pals had committed suicide after a long battle with a terminal illness. Susan and I figured Phil might try the same.

One sunny spring afternoon after a visit, Susan and I were outside talking. A gun went off from the direction of the house. We shot in there, only to find Phil sitting there smiling, wondering what the hubbub was about. Some guy just fired off his rifle was all, not a thing to get worked up about. It only grabs your attention if you think you might know who was on the barrel end of it. In this case it was probably just a gopher.

For all of his talk about the old days, Phil was in fact a closet progressive. He was a lifelong Democrat, and he let professors from Montana State University run fertilization tests on his wheat ground. Phil had become one of the first farmers in the area to take fertilizing crops seriously. It paid off for him. Lots of people considered him one of the best farmers in the valley.

So one time when he threw his "a little religion goes a *lawng* way" line at me, I responded with "Yeah, I agree, but you know, a little fertilizer goes a long way too. Too much nitrogen burns the roots, or it makes it all stalk and no head, but the right amount does a lot of good. Religion is like that. It isn't all bad. Too much'll do you in, but every soul needs a little."

He laughed loudly and slapped his knee—which is another really fine compliment—because he knew I'd got him good. Deep down he wanted me to do that. He wouldn't have respected me if I couldn't return a barb now and then. So he let me read the Bible to him and tell him about Jesus and pray for him. And whereas most of my parishioners find that kind of thing a tad boring, with Phil, reading a Bible verse and a prayer made him cry. Even though he was right about too much religion, his soul was starved for gospel nutrients.

Phil died. He never packed in a lot of religion, but he got enough of Jesus to make the trip. He'll never know how much I agreed with him that "a little religion goes a *lawng* way." Only a preacher can really know what that means.

Sabbath and Religion

People with too much religion in them—including preachers— are souls polluted by rules, regulations and religious experiences, which they interpret as norms for everyone. They think they know how every Christian ought to live and what every minister should and shouldn't do. They want to regulate how people think.

Souls function right with emptiness and freedom. Overreligious people are not empty and they are not free, and they abhor emptiness and freedom in others.

I'm not in favor of spiritual anarchy or moral relativism. Some people consider me overreligious because I believe the Ten Commandments are normative for Christians. But trying to live by the Ten Commandments isn't overreligion. Overreligion is believing that the corollaries implied by the Ten Commandments carry the same weight as the commandments themselves.

Anyone who cares about the Ten Commandments interprets them for practical, daily life. However, our interpretations, reasonable as they may be, are just that, extrapolations, and not the real thing. A good example of a command subject to interpretation is the sabbath command. It goes like this:

Remember the sabbath day, and keep it holy. Six days you shall labor and do all your work. But the seventh day is a sabbath to the LORD your God; you shall not do any work—you, your son or your daughter, your male or female slave, your livestock, or the alien resident in your towns. For in six days the LORD made heaven and earth, the sea, and all that is in them, but rested the seventh day; therefore the LORD blessed the sabbath day and consecrated it. (Ex 20:8-11)

What does the commandment say, and what does it imply? It says we need to take a day off from work each week and dedicate that day to the Lord. I imply from it that I need to go to church every Sunday and that I should avoid work as much as possible on that day. When I was in college and graduate school I didn't study on Sundays. That worked for me. Does that mean that everyone should hear the commandment that way? I doubt it.

In our valley we have a large, conservative Dutch community. Many of them farm. They leaven our valley with a positive Christian witness, but sometimes it goes a little too far. As a community under the Word of God, they strive to observe the Lord's sabbath. On Sundays most do the minimum amount of work required to keep their animals healthy. Most will not harvest on Sunday. Most of them are wealthy. They try to exercise some control over what goes on in their community on Sundays.

Some years ago, a parishioner of ours, a Presbyterian, delivered the Sunday-morning paper to the Dutch people just before daylight on the Lord's Day. The Dutch farmers used to go out and get their paper and read it before church. But the Dutch elders considered reading the newspaper before worship on the Lord's Day to be less than proper observance. So they asked the brother to kindly deliver the paper after church.

Well, this fellow was a farmer himself, he had a family, he had worship to attend, and the last thing he wanted to do on a sweet Sunday afternoon was deliver newspapers. So he asked the Dutch elders if they wouldn't mind asking their people to leave the newspaper in the roadside box until after Sunday worship. They had little choice but to agree, since none of *them* would deliver the newspaper on Sunday. Presumably, many of the Dutch farmers were glad that the paper continued to be delivered before first light.

In their defense, the elders were simply trying to enforce norms for community behavior in order to preserve the religious heritage and cultural identity of a distinct people living in an invasive, secular cultural environment. That's the good motive which initiates a lot of our overreligion. It begins as a project to preserve the soul of a community by protecting the souls of its people from worldly pollution. Unfortunately, the very rules and norms intended to protect us from the world quickly become religious-worldly pollution.

The apostle Paul calls these rules "elemental spirits of the universe." He tells the Christians in Colossae,

If with Christ you died to the elemental spirits of the universe, why do you live as if you still belonged to the world? Why do you submit to regulations, "Do not handle, Do not taste, Do not touch"? All these regulations refer to things that perish with use; they are simply human commands and teachings. These have indeed an appearance of wisdom in promoting self-imposed piety, humility, and severe treatment of the body, but they are of no value in checking self-indulgence. (Col 2:20-23)

This is very much to the point with regard to the soul, because often we equate building up the soul with stricter discipline and following more rules. Of course some souls do need more discipline and a few more rules. Ten would be enough—but we can't stop there. If ten are good, twenty would be better, and fifty better still.

Rules kill. Overreligion packs the soul so tight there's no room for the Spirit of God, for the freedom requisite to responsibility, for space that permits light, shadow, inquiry and beauty. Rules and regulations pollute a soul the way silt pollutes a river. It asphyxiates spirit. Tightly packed overreligion is what Jesus fought the Pharisees over. It's what hung him on the cross.

Jesus' Battle with the Pharisees

Who the Pharisees were. The Pharisees were good guys trying to do good things. Until we grasp how much we would have admired them if we had lived in their day, and how much we admire

Christian Pharisees today, we can't really understand the battle Jesus fought with them. The Pharisees were laymen, largely middle-class types, with connections in the social world above them and the social world below them. Their mark in history comes from their battle with Jesus, but they didn't fight just with Jesus. They participated in an ongoing debate between factions of Judaism in the first-century Roman world.

First-century Judaism was not a monolithic structure but rather a loose confederation of schools and groups of thought and practice. Three of those groups were the Sadducees, the Pharisees and the Essenes. The Sadducees were a powerful, upper-crust mainline group. The Essenes (creators of the Dead Sea scrolls) were an exclusivistic, reclusive sect. The Pharisees thought the Sadducees had sold out to Greco-Roman culture, and the Essenes thought both the Pharisees and the Sadducees had sold out. The Pharisees and the Sadducees thought the Essenes were off in their own little world and no real good to anyone.

The Pharisees were in many ways the centrist group, the "evangelicals" in today's terms, with strong practical ties to the common people, who greatly admired them. Their teachings centered on everyday personal, religious issues like how to wash your hands correctly according to the law of Moses. They had strong feelings about how the sabbath ought to be observed. (Sort of like if and when it is OK to read the newspaper on the Lord's Day.) They tended to be extremely careful about whom they shared fellowship with, corresponding to their rigid boundaries for who was in and who was out of God's covenant people.

To their credit, theirs was not a self-help movement. Pharisaism was eschatological. They believed the world teetered toward the end times and the Day of God's righteous judgment could be hastened by right living among God's people. Though we think of their overreligion as overjudgmental, they viewed human beings optimistically. They believed in the goodness of God's law. They believed people could change for the better, and society could change for the better, if everyone simply followed God's law (their way). They weren't paid. They worked regular jobs, cared for families and gave a lot of time to their mission of improving the spiritual and moral discipline of the common people. If the Pharisees had gathered together to write a mission statement, it might read something like this: "To promote practical, daily righteousness in God's people through personal example, public teaching, mentoring disciples and rigorous social awareness, and so hasten the coming Day of the Lord."

What's wrong that? Not much. The German New Testament scholar Leonhard Goppelt tells us the Pharisees "represented the highest standard of excellence that he [Jesus] could find in Israel."[1] That they executed their mission imperfectly, with hypocrisy and legalism, makes them no different from Christian ministries today. And like many Christian ministries today, despite their failings, they accomplished a lot of good. So praise the Lord. And pass the ammunition.

What Jesus and the Pharisees fought over. Jesus grew up saturated in Pharisaic piety. His immediate and extended family probably sympathized with the Pharisaic mission. It is easy to imagine that Joseph and Mary knew some Pharisees personally and that some of Jesus' boyhood acquaintances became Pharisees as adults.

It wasn't a bad life. But for Jesus, growing up in a subculture like Pharisaic Judaism bent him not to conformity but to informed protest. He knew the Pharisaic hot buttons, and he wasn't afraid to push them. From the beginning of his work, it became apparent that the Pharisees needed to loosen their boundaries to account for the new work of God in his ministry. Some Pharisees did. As a movement they did not. Jesus struggled with the Pharisees over the interpretation of the Mosaic law on two primary issues, the sabbath command and who was in and who was out.

Jesus' disagreements with the Pharisees over the sabbath were like the continental divide. They started at the same point, but their arguments flowed like rivers in opposite directions toward two different oceans of thought. Jesus taught sabbath as intended for human good, as a sign of freedom and rest. He could not impose it as a burden. To make his point, one sabbath Jesus and his disciples, in view of some Pharisees, snapped off some heads of grain as they walked along a field. This act broke sabbath in the Pharisaic mind. Another time he healed a man with a shriveled hand in synagogue on the sabbath. These violations infuriated the Pharisees. Jesus embarrassed them in both events by showing that their extrapolations regarding the sabbath command were burdensome, inhumane and ludicrous.

Liberalizing the sabbath command provoked the Pharisees because strict sabbath observance was a major plank in their platform of reform. The sabbath wasn't just one of the Mosaic laws, it was the law that symbolized all the rest. It represented covenant life in its highest form, and it pointed to life in Paradise. They weren't just unhappy fundamentalists who couldn't bear imagining someone having a good time on Saturday. To their way of thinking, Jesus' relatively nonchalant attitude toward sabbath threatened the national future of Judaism. So early in his ministry they began plotting with political leaders about getting rid of him (Mk 2:23—3:6).

Jesus made friends with sinners. He got real chummy with the kind of people the Pharisees were determined to either convert or discredit. Furthermore, his dalliances with Palestinian lowlifes lacked public discretion. He walked right up a tax collector. Instead of knifing him, which is what a lot of the religious people would have liked to have had the guts to do, he talked with him and even asked him to be his disciple. The fed agreed and promptly invited Jesus to a party at his house. There Jesus ate and drank with a large and fascinating collection of religiously undisciplined people. The Pharisees watched from the outside. And burned.

By befriending sinners, Jesus erased the boundaries between those the Pharisees taught were accepted by God and those they were quite certain he rejected. Since Jesus was an acknowledged teacher and miracle worker within the Pharisaic tradition, his friendship with sinners threatened the fabric of the Pharisaic subculture. By cavorting with deviants, Jesus fuzzied up the boundaries.

In the world the Pharisees envisioned, boundaries were important, and they required maintenance. This instinct typifies religious subcultures characterized by overreligion and eschatological dreams. In a book on social deviancy in Puritan New England, *Wayward Puritans,* Kai Erikson tells us that "deviant forms of behavior, by marking the outer edges of group life, give the inner structure its special character and thus supply the framework within which the people of the group develop an orderly sense of their own cultural identity."[2] Jesus represented to the Pharisees what witchcraft represented to the leaders of the Massachusetts Bay Colony: a grave threat to their social and spiritual revival, which aimed at nothing less than the transformation of the world. From their perspective the only way to preserve the cogency of the mission was to punish miscreants publicly. Through such exemplification of their deviancy, the social and moral boundaries might be reestablished.

The Pharisees and their professional religious counterparts the scribes didn't crucify Jesus alone. The Sadducees and the priests had their role to play, and the Romans were not innocent bystanders. Nevertheless, Jesus' struggle with the Pharisees catalyzed the battle with the entire Palestinian authority structure, creating allies of sworn enemies.

Jesus probably would have agreed that "a little religion goes a *lawng* way." In any case, it was people chock-full of religion who crucified him.

In fairness to the Pharisees, Jesus of Nazareth would have clashed with the best people of any society, of any religion, and he still does. The crucified and risen Lord Jesus confounds human goodness all around the world through the preaching of the gospel of the cross. Paul calls preaching Christ crucified "a stumbling block to Jews and foolishness to Gentiles, but to those who are the called, both Jews and Greeks, Christ the power of God and the wisdom of God" (1 Cor 1:23-24). "For Jesus' cross is essentially directed against all religious illusion and relegates man to man's humanity."[3] Facing the humanness of our humanity is precisely what the overreligious soul will not do and cannot do, since it truly believes it can assert itself over and against God, with its impressive efforts to follow God's law.

It was precisely a monumental human effort to reach God that became the foil for the salvific act, so that "every mouth may be silenced, and the whole world may be held accountable to God" (Rom 3:19).

The Soul of Jesus at the Cross

That Jesus fuzzied up the boundaries between who was in and who was out cannot be disputed. Paul, a former Pharisee, takes it much further. To his mind Jesus not only fellowshipped with sinners, risking pollution, but took the pollution on himself. He became more than an outcast: he became the pollution. Paul tells us, "For our sake [God] made him to be sin who knew no sin, so that in him we might become the righteousness of God" (2 Cor 5:21). He is saying that on the cross God the Father made God the Son to be sin so that by condemning sin in the person of his Son, he might make us the righteousness of God.

To understand this—insofar as we can—we need to consider the divine and human nature of Jesus Christ. This was the other arena of battle between Jesus and the Pharisees, for Jesus claimed a unique relationship with God.

In one of his early miracles, recorded in the Gospel according to Mark, Jesus was teaching in a crowded room. Some fellows, hearing of his power to heal, brought their paralyzed friend to the house, hoping to present him to Jesus for healing. The house was packed as tightly with bodies as the souls of the Pharisees were packed with rules and regulations. So these men, undaunted by the human jam, climbed on the house, tore the roof open and lowered their friend, still on his pallet, into the room in front of God and everyone.

Jesus didn't heal him right away. There was a hot button to push. He simply told the man, "Son, your sins are forgiven." Jesus knew the scribes and Pharisees would think, "Why does this fellow speak in this way? It is blasphemy! Who can forgive sins but God alone?" (Mk 2:5-7). His point exactly. Then to show that his authority to forgive carried a Spirit-filled knockout punch, Jesus healed the man and sent him on his way.

An early Christian hymn Paul uses in his letter to the Philippians summarizes the incarnation of Christ succinctly:

Who, though he was in the form of God,
did not regard equality with God
as something to be exploited,
but emptied himself,
taking the form of a slave,
being born in human likeness.
And being found in human form,
he humbled himself
and became obedient to the point of death —
even death on a cross. (Phil 2:6-8)

The divine Son of God, Jesus of Nazareth, was fully human in body and in soul. Maybe it's easier to grasp that he was fully human in body than that he was fully human in soul. Yet the soul of Jesus was human, and as such was as mortal and as vulnerable as ours. The Spirit breathed his soul just as the Spirit breathes ours. His soul was emptier than ours. That is, whereas our souls are packed with every whim and spirit of greed, good, religion, lust and love; his was a vast, open cathedral filled with the Spirit of God, with whom he communed in faith.

How could this soul become sin? How could he *become sin* without *becoming sinful?*

God the Father laid the stinking, cold, wet blanket of our war with him, in all its hideous forms, religious and irreligious, on the warm, pulsing life of Jesus. Sin sank in, chilling his flesh and bone and soul, until he could taste the rotten wetness on his tongue. As he died, God's holy wrath expended itself on that sin, in the body and the soul of Jesus—we cannot help but think, *especially* in his soul.

The Gospels tell us that "at three o'clock Jesus cried out with a loud voice, 'Eloi, Eloi, lema sabachthani?' which means, 'My God, my God, why have you forsaken me?' " (Mk 15:34). His mortal soul, so empty for God, cried in pain as he slowly filled with the wretched fluid of "the great wine press of the wrath of God" (Rev 14:19). Then his soul, heavy with indignation, dropped from his body into hell.[4]

Thus the word of the prophet was fulfilled:

He was wounded for our transgressions,
  crushed for our iniquities;
upon him was the punishment that made us whole,
  and by his bruises we are healed. (Is 53:5)

Resurrection

On the third day Jesus rose from the grave, alive in resurrection splendor. What is resurrection life? Our ideas about life after death vary so widely that it is perhaps best to begin by saying what resurrection life is not.

Resurrection life is not a ghost existence. Jesus did not become a ghost or a wandering spirit. The disciples were terrified of ghosts. They would not have considered Jesus' return to them in the form of a ghost as good news in any sense. Old Testament laws against interacting with spirits were strict!

Not a resuscitation. In resuscitation a dead, or almost dead, human body is brought back to life. A resuscitated life is the same body, alive in the same way, in the same world. A resuscitated body is immediately subject to disease and decay as before. Everyone resuscitated eventually dies again, permanently. A resurrection body cannot die. It is not subject to disease, decay or death. It is physical, but it does not degenerate.

Not a reincarnation. Reincarnation is the belief that the souls of the dead return to the earth, where they come back to life joined with new bodies. Reincarnation life is an endless succession of lives, bodies and deaths. Reincarnation is not taught in the Bible. It is, to be quite frank, a poor belief system. For one thing, under the terms of reincarnation we die thousands, even millions, of times. The Bible teaches that we die once, twice I guess if you happen to be resuscitated. As it is, resuscitated people often report not wanting to come back—who wants to die again?

Furthermore, reincarnation is cruel because it teaches that

poor and oppressed people are born into their plight due to sins in past lives. The Bible teaches that poverty and injustice exist because human power structures refuse just stewardship of resources. It shouldn't be too difficult to see why reincarnation is in vogue among wealthy and powerful people in our world today. It justifies their wealth, power and stature. It is difficult, however, to reconcile how previous lives of righteousness could lead to reincarnated lives of rank self-indulgence.

What resurrection life is. Paul gives the Christians in Corinth a glimpse of the mystery of the resurrected body when he tells them,

> What I am saying, brothers and sisters, is this: flesh and blood cannot inherit the kingdom of God, nor does the perishable inherit the imperishable. Listen, I will tell you a mystery! We will not all die, but we will all be changed, in a moment, in the twinkling of an eye, at the last trumpet. For the trumpet will sound, and the dead will be raised imperishable, and we will be changed. For this perishable body must put on imperishability, and this mortal body must put on immortality. When this perishable body puts on imperishability, and this mortal body puts on immortality, then the saying that is written will be fulfilled: "Death has been swallowed up in victory." (1 Cor 15:50-54)

Following Jesus into resurrection life in the new heavens and the new earth is the ultimate hope for all Christians and for the whole world. Resurrection life is without religion. All human striving toward God is over. The prophet of Apocalypse tells us of life in this new world: "I saw no temple in the city, for its temple is the Lord God the Almighty and the Lamb. And the city has no need of sun or moon to shine on it, for the glory of God is its light, and its lamp is the Lamb" (Rev 21:22-23).

War is over, and so is all killing. The prophet Isaiah recounts for us the vision his soul sees:

> The wolf shall live with the lamb,
>> the leopard shall lie down with the kid,
> the calf and the lion and the fatling together,

and a little child shall lead them.
The cow and the bear shall graze,
  their young shall lie down together;
  and the lion shall eat straw like the ox.
The nursing child shall play over the hole of the asp,
  and the weaned child shall put its hand on the adder's den.
They will not hurt or destroy
  on all my holy mountain;
for the earth will be full of the knowledge of the LORD
  as the waters cover the sea. (Is 11:6-9)

This is a world of peace and life, without death, tears or pain. If this is incomprehensible to us, it is because our souls are so full of death and pain there is simply too little room for dreams. But "in the last days it will be, God declares, that I will pour out my Spirit upon all flesh, and your sons and your daughters shall prophesy, and your young men shall see visions, and your old men shall dream dreams" (Acts 2:17). These Spirit visions of life as it can be fill the empty soul with music and praise.

The Faith Paradigm for Soul Cure

In the meantime, "a little religion goes a *lawng* way." If our best attempts at religious reform are enough to send the Son of God to the cross, it should be plain that we need a paradigm of soul cure other than the Pharisaic/legalistic/religious project of social and spiritual control. We need a paradigm of soul cure based not in what we do for our own sick souls but on what God has done for us in the death and resurrection of Christ, applied by the direct work of God on the soul.

The work of God is received on our part by faith, which is the soul's original and only possible relation to God. In his essay "The Freedom of the Christian," Martin Luther describes beautifully the transaction that takes place between the soul and Christ in the act of faith.

The . . . incomparable benefit of faith is that it unites the soul with Christ as a bride is united with her bridegroom. By this mystery, the Apostle teaches, Christ and the soul become one flesh (Ephesians 5:31-32). And if they are one flesh and there is between them a true marriage—indeed the most perfect of all marriages, since human marriages are but poor examples of this one true marriage—it follows that everything they have they hold in common, the good as well as the evil. Accordingly the believing soul can boast and glory in whatever Christ has as though it were his own, and whatever the soul has Christ claims as his own. Let us compare these and we shall see inestimable benefits. Christ is full of grace, life and salvation. The soul is full of sins, death and damnation. Now let faith come between them and sins, death and damnation will be Christ's while grace, life and salvation will be the soul's; for if Christ is the bridegroom, he must take upon himself the things which are the bride's and bestow upon her the things that are his. If he gives her his body and very self, how shall he not give her all that is his? And if he takes the body of the bride, how shall he not take all that is hers?[5]

Eleven

Dying & Rising
with Christ

••

*I*n faith union with Christ, our souls claim all that belongs to
Christ: grace, life and salvation. Christ in return claims all that
belongs to us: sins, death and damnation.

This metaphor of our faith union with Christ is drawn from
marriage. Another metaphor for this grand transaction is perhaps
more well known, the metaphor of rebirth. Jesus told the Pharisee Nicodemus that he must be reborn (Jn 3:3). What happens
in the new birth? Jesus tells dumbfounded Nicodemus, "The
wind blows where it chooses, and you hear the sound of it, but
you do not know where it comes from or where it goes. So it is
with everyone who is born of the Spirit" (Jn 3:8).

The new birth is a work of the Spirit of God, but specifically
it is a work of the Spirit of the crucified and risen Savior. Paul
the former Pharisee also uses the metaphor of rebirth to describe
the faith union with Christ when he tells the Corinthian Christians, "So if anyone is in Christ, there is a new creation: every-

thing old has passed away; see, everything has become new!" (2 Cor 5:17).

In rebirth, the breath of life becomes the breath of the crucified and risen Lord Jesus. In this process the Holy Spirit of the crucified and risen Lord Jesus regenerates the soul into the event-image of Jesus. The soul's "I am" becomes the cry of the Son to the Father by the Holy Spirit. As Paul says, "God has sent the Spirit of his Son into our hearts, crying, 'Abba! Father!' " (Gal 4:6).

All human souls are generated in the image of God. In Christ we are *re*generated in the image of the divine Son of God, and specifically in the image of his death and resurrection. Regeneration is not simply the presence of the Spirit of Jesus Christ regenerating the soul; it is the presence of the *crucified and resurrected Jesus* regenerating the soul. The soul is regenerated when the historic act of salvation becomes real in the life of the regenerate. The new life in Christ is the personal/historic process of becoming Christlike in faith union with him.

In his essay "Dying and Rising with Christ," Roman Catholic New Testament scholar Rudolf Schnackenburg says, "The Christian is one who has been drawn into the event of the crucifixion. At the same time the life of Christ, the risen Lord, becomes operative in the Christian: no longer is it his own ego, but Christ himself living in him."[1] Our life process of rebirth and new life in Christ in which the soul is regenerated into the image of Christ is not an easy road. Paul and Barnabas told a group of new Christians, "It is through many persecutions that we must enter the kingdom of God" (Acts 14:22). A man I scarce dare call my friend, the honor is so great, exemplifies in the extreme the meaning of dying and rising with Christ.

Calvin

A man institutionalized twice for mental illness was the sanest person I ever knew. His commitments were not mistakes. He needed custodial protection to stay alive while something inside him died so that something inside him could live.

Calvin's first pastorate chewed him into raw meat. Since I loved the man, I happen to think no church was worthy of him. But that may not be true. Probably a church existed that would have accepted his love and cared for his need. In those days, however, churches began abandoning modesty. As they became conscious of power and unafraid to handle it, it was inevitable that a few poor souls would touch the ark in an attempt to keep the church from going in the ditch. Today he blames no one. He admits he made mistakes his first time out, but it goes deeper than a few mistakes here and there.

Following World War II, he studied at a seminary whose anthropology was grandfatherly. It suited him. A theology that all people are good and will outgrow imperfections given love and education made sense to his naturally kind heart. Unfortunately, this theology, nurtured in academia during a time when the world seemed as if it was getting better, hit the churches at a time when the world was getting worse. Paul Tillich taught the ground of all being, Humphrey Bogart taught the groundlessness of all being. Church people flocked to both, and Bogart got the Oscar. *Love* became a four-letter synonym for *power.* The churches understood it, but Calvin didn't.

That wasn't how his mother raised him. Calvin inherited his mother's love, and her dread of sin. He consciously embraced her love. He tried rejecting her traditional view of sin, thinking it an anachronism incompatible with higher learning, but he could only repress it. A mother's dread of sin is tough to disinherit. So it controlled him from the inside, while his happy theology of sin as lack of knowledge paralyzed his ministry with real live sinners. The church violated him, but he didn't have the intellectual tools to recognize it. He internalized it, blaming himself. If not for the genetic strike against him, he might have withstood the blows and even returned some, but his fists were paralyzed.

He never talked much about his dad. Not because there wasn't much to say. His dad labored and provided. He was no drinker, but he lived in a subdued state, always around but never quite there. From his father Calvin received an indefatigable capacity for work and depression. Calvin vaguely remembers his father's stint in a mental institution during Calvin's childhood. But like Calvin, his father kept at life and faith. He was active in church work, wrote and distributed evangelical tracts, and was a hymn writer. He constructed his own coffin twenty years before he died.

His mother lived in outward love, his father in inward passion. Their respective systems served each fairly well, and they lived reasonably happy lives, certainly godly lives. Calvin took up the best of both, with the depression, and the combination proved nearly fatal.

The actual details of his first parish are not clear to me, because frankly they were not particularly clear to Calvin himself. One thing's for sure: he worked himself silly. He was not married. There was no one at home to stomp a foot and demand a sabbath rest. He believed implicitly in hard work, whether he was pounding nails or driving home a point in a sermon. Pounding nails may be healthy for people with depression, but pastoral ministry crushes a tender spirit.

Most of Calvin's parishioners loved him, but some viewed him as weak. I once knew a girl who walked with leg braces. One afternoon on her way home from school she hobbled down an alley past a Doberman pinscher behind an eight-foot fence. The dog jumped the fence and chewed her up real bad. Calvin's experience was like that. Some Doberman parishioners went after him like he was in braces. In almost every church there are a few sick people who brutalize frail leaders. This has been going on for a long time.

In the first century some of the brothers and sisters in the church in Corinth looked down on the apostle Paul for his weaknesses. Paul had founded the church. When he left Corinth to preach the gospel elsewhere, he entrusted the church to gifted men and women of faith. Eventually the Corinthian church, never long on modesty, allowed leadership to fall into the hands of religious power porkers Paul called "super-apostles" (2 Cor 11:5), "false apostles" and "deceitful workers" (11:13). These

"Christians" attacked Paul viciously on the issue of his frailties. They claimed he was not a great preacher (10:10) — a point on which Paul was in agreement. They recognized the weight of his letters but said that in person he was timid and unimpressive (10:10). They criticized him for his physical problems (12:7-9). He was supposedly a man of great signs and wonders: why was he still sick? Did he have enough faith? Did he have spiritual power? Was he really an apostle?

Paul defended the legitimacy of his suffering. He offered no excuses. The letters he wrote from prison[2] don't sound like Job or Ecclesiastes. They are instead his happiest writings. In Paul's eyes his suffering was his glory. He did not cower before his opponents' health, strength and skills. He claimed his weakness was part of God's election. As he tells the Corinthians,

> He said to me, "My grace is sufficient for you, for power is made perfect in weakness." So, I will boast all the more gladly of my weaknesses, so that the power of Christ may dwell in me. Therefore I am content with weaknesses, insults, hardships, persecutions, and calamities for the sake of Christ; for whenever I am weak, then I am strong. (2 Cor 12:9-10)

He names and claims suffering as vital to his ministry. "For just as the sufferings of Christ are abundant for us, so also our consolation is abundant through Christ. If we are being afflicted, it is for your consolation and salvation; if we are being consoled, it is for your consolation, which you experience when you patiently endure the same sufferings that we are also suffering" (1:5-6). On one level this is a psychological defense of suffering: a person who has experienced pain can identify with a fellow sufferer. Paul recognizes this, but he means much more. For in his suffering as an apostle, Paul believes that he and those who work with him are "always carrying in the body the death of Jesus, so that the life of Jesus may also be made visible in our bodies. For while we live, we are always being given up to death for Jesus' sake, so that the life of Jesus may be made visible in our mortal flesh. So death is at work in us, but life in you" (2 Cor 4:10-12).

Paul's ministry was attacked precisely at the point at which it had the most to offer: Christ. The Corinthians wanted power-filled religion more than Christlike ministry.

Jesus, Paul and Calvin suffered most in their work at the hands of the people of God. If any of the three had abandoned the people of God, they would have suffered less but they would have abandoned their call, leaving their appointed path of sanctification and glory. Every prophet in the Old Testament faced the same dilemma. Furthermore, the subtext of every book in the New Testament is the particular, blessed suffering each writer endured to write inspired by the Holy Spirit. That we gain life from what they suffered is their election to the imitation of Christ on our behalf.

It may be too strong to suggest that Calvin's church had a demon, though I believe some churches do have demons, and maybe this one did. Anyway, he ended up something like the man in the Gospel story who lived among the graves. Calvin didn't go around naked, breaking chains, but he was definitely beside himself. He required twenty-four-hour protection.

He did not rejoin pastoral ministry per se. He married and became a businessman. He managed people well. His bent for efficiency coupled with concern for the welfare of his employees made him quite successful. The business world rewarded his work ethic, but his soul couldn't take it. He labored himself into a second institutionalization, after which he returned to business. For the rest of his life he split his energies between ministry to his employees and ministry to ministers.

He suffered depression the rest of his life. Some mornings he couldn't get out of bed. At times he wept for reasons apparent to no one including himself. I give his doctors credit. He survived. They made his lifelong battle for peace possible. Five sets of electroshock therapy, consistent psychotherapy and later, as they became available, psychotherapeutic drugs kept Calvin alive. He never got well. He was never going to get well. His doctors kept him pieced together. He never got fixed, but Christ raised him from the dead many times.

Rising with Christ

Paul revealed to the Christians in Galatia, "It is no longer I who live, but it is Christ who lives in me" (Gal 2:20). That was Calvin in the days I knew him. Strength emanated from the center of his soul, but you would have had a hard time calling it ego strength. The power was sweet and peaceful, and you didn't mess with it. When you considered fighting him, the cost always seemed too high. He was a man with little to lose that he hadn't already lost and regained once or twice over. I freely admit that his humility frightened me more than once. His transparency concealed a holy flame.

The fire within was Jesus' presence in Calvin's prayer. The Spirit of Jesus prayed within him, for him and for those he loved.

I was alone in the sanctuary Tuesday afternoon. I walked down the aisle and I stopped at every pew and I prayed for each person that normally sits in that row . . . there is so much need, so much pain. I pleaded for God's blessing upon every family. Where a need was known to me I prayed for it specifically; when I didn't know the situation I prayed God's peace into their lives.

I resigned my position on the church council. Having served off and on for thirty years I feel I have a new role to play now. I asked our pastor if I could stay in a back room of the church while the council meets and pray for the meeting. I didn't know what he would think of that idea, but he seemed pleased. I hold our pastor up for prayer every day as well.

More and more I am being called by the Lord to play with children. I am no longer a lay leader; instead I volunteer for nursery. I just sit in the middle of the room and play with them. It is wonderful.

God gifted Calvin to protect and encourage pastors. No pastor failed in ministry during Calvin's thirty years on council. He prayed for them, encouraged them, admonishing if necessary, and generally steered them clear of trouble. When conflict occurred, he was there to mediate, and if the situation demanded he "set his face like a flint" toward the obdurate. Few stood in his way. The church and its pastors accepted his love and cared for his need, for he remained a needy man, but in return they gained the presence of Jesus.

The bargain was all theirs. Knowing him, one met Jesus. For he had died and risen with Christ, and he no longer lived, but Christ lived in him. The spiritual fact is that Calvin became a regenerated man. He was reborn. His soul became one breathed by Jesus, baptized in his death and resurrection.

Crucifying the Flesh

Just watch a Christian television station for five minutes, and you will realize that regeneration does not increase a person's intelligence. Regeneration does not make a violinist better at playing the violin or a carpenter better at framing. Regeneration does not make hair grow back. So what good is it?

If regeneration made us smarter, better and prettier, we ought to pray for the regeneration of animals as well as human beings. I've seen some cats that I felt could use a lot of help. But animals do not need regeneration. Even the Doberman that slashed the face of my little friend in braces didn't need regeneration. The dog's owner needed regeneration. Not one contrite word came from his mouth. The dog was his weapon.

Animals have bodies and souls, but they do not sin. Humans have bodies and souls, and they do sin. Sin dwells in the soul—as opposed to fingers and arteries—so regeneration deals with the soul.

But two classic New Testament texts, typifying others, seem to indicate otherwise. First of course are Jesus' horrifying images of eye removal and hand separation.

You have heard that it was said, "You shall not commit adultery." But I say to you that everyone who looks at a woman with lust has already committed adultery with her in his heart. If your right eye causes you to sin, tear it out and throw it away; it is better for you to lose one of your members than for your whole body to be thrown into hell. And if your right hand causes you to sin, cut it off and throw it away; it is better for you to lose one of your members than for your whole body to go into hell. (Mt 5:27-30)

Does Jesus mean that the eye is responsible for lust and the hand is responsible for stealing?

Does Paul intend essentially the same thing in contrasting the "works of the flesh" and the "fruit of the Spirit"?

Now the works of the flesh are obvious: fornication, impurity, licentiousness, idolatry, sorcery, enmities, strife, jealousy, anger, quarrels, dissensions, factions, envy, drunkenness, carousing, and things like these. I am warning you, as I warned you before: those who do such things will not inherit the kingdom of God.

By contrast, the fruit of the Spirit is love, joy, peace, patience, kindness, generosity, faithfulness, gentleness, and self-control. There is no law against such things. And those who belong to Christ Jesus have crucified the flesh with its passions and desires. (Gal 5:19-24)

The New International Version, a modern Bible translation with a "concern for clear and natural English,"[3] translates *flesh* as "sinful nature." "Sinful nature" isn't as grand stylistically as simply *flesh*, and it isn't as literal a translation of the Greek word Paul used *(sarx)*, but it may communicate better to a modern audience what Paul meant.

Ironically, Paul assists our understanding of what he means by the "works of the flesh" in prescribing a cure for the problem of sin far more gruesome than the one Jesus gives. Whereas Jesus advises us to gouge out an eye or cut off a hand as needed, Paul's suggestion goes the whole route: he says the *flesh* must be crucified. He tells us that "those who belong to Christ Jesus have crucified the flesh" (Gal 5:24).

Common sense, one of our best allies in biblical interpretation, makes it perfectly clear that Jesus did not teach dismemberment and Paul did not teach self-crucifixion. However, Jesus did teach that because of sin something needs to be cut off. From Paul's perspective, something needs to be crucified. Some part of us must be cut off or killed so that the person God created us to be can live.

A Circumcised Heart

The most important ritual of the Old Testament is also about cutting something so that the whole person can live. This is the rite of circumcision, the cutting off of the foreskin of the penis. Hundreds of years before Moses and the Ten Commandments, God told Abraham, "This is my covenant, which you shall keep, between me and you and your offspring after you: Every male among you shall be circumcised. You shall circumcise the flesh of your foreskins, and it shall be a sign of the covenant between me and you" (Gen 17:10-11). The penalty for refusing circumcision was great: "Any uncircumcised male who is not circumcised in the flesh of his foreskin shall be cut off from his people; he has broken my covenant" (v. 14).

Circumcision symbolized a cutting off from covenant fellowship with the Lord and with his covenant people. Cutting off the foreskin symbolized cutting off life. The covenant worked like this: Follow God's covenant statutes, and you and your family will live with the Lord God and with the people of God. Fail to keep the covenant statutes, and what is symbolized by circumcision will happen to you.

The physical rite of circumcision remained in force throughout Old Testament times and throughout all Jewish history. Later in Old Testament times the physical rite, still practiced, took on a spiritual reinterpretation that also remained normative for Judaism. The symbolism shifted from the penis to the heart. Literal circumcision was still practiced, but the intention was that the heart would be circumcised. "Circumcise, then, the foreskin of your heart, and do not be stubborn any longer" (Deut 10:16).

The circumcision of the heart became a matter of prophetic warning:

Circumcise yourselves to the LORD,
   remove the foreskin of your hearts,
   O people of Judah and inhabitants of Jerusalem,
or else my wrath will go forth like fire,
   and burn with no one to quench it,
   because of the evil of your doings. (Jer 4:4)

It became a matter of prophetic hope: "Moreover, the LORD your God will circumcise your heart and the heart of your descendants, so that you will love the LORD your God with all your heart and with all your soul, in order that you may live" (Deut 30:6). So Paul teaches nothing new when he tells the Christians in Rome, "For a person is not a Jew who is one outwardly, nor is true circumcision something external and physical. Rather, a person is a Jew who is one inwardly, and real circumcision is a matter of the heart—it is spiritual and not literal" (Rom 2:28-29).

The same is true of Jesus' injunction to gouge out one's eye and cut off one's hand, and Paul's hope-filled declaration that we crucify our flesh. The interpretation in each case *is spiritual and not literal.* The crucifixion of the flesh is spiritual because the works of the flesh spring from evil in the heart. Paul's injunction that the flesh be crucified corresponds to the Old Testament injunction that the heart be circumcised.

Baptism: Becoming Human

In the New Testament baptism replaces the Old Testament rite of circumcision. Baptism's vast advantage over circumcision is in its second half. The first half of baptism symbolizes essentially the same thing as the whole of circumcision: death, the cutting off of life. We go into the water; this symbolizes entry into death. Whereas in circumcision the rite is finished after death is symbolized, in baptism death is only the beginning. In the second half of baptism we come out of the water. Coming up out of the water symbolizes resurrection out of death into life.

Furthermore, we are baptized in the name of the Father and in the name of the Son and in the name of the Holy Spirit. We are not alone. In baptism we die with Jesus and live with Jesus. It is the tomb of Jesus that we enter, and it is the resurrection of Jesus that disgorges us out of death into life.

Calvin was baptized into the death of Jesus and out of death into the life of Jesus. His baptism symbolized the work of God in his life: he died and Jesus lived. In one sense it was finished in a moment. Jesus entered into his life in faith. In another sense the dying and rising occurred over his entire life.

Lives like Calvin's reveal precious little about human decision, discipline and rituals; there is little to say at all about what Calvin did or did not do. I can't tell you what he did that turned his suffering into sweetness compared with others whose suffering degenerates into hellish bitterness.

Paul told the Christians in Colossae, "For you have died, and your life is hidden with Christ in God" (Col 3:3). Determining what God does and what we do in the Christian life is fruitless and pointless. Good souls hold many different theologies but one faith: "Every generous act of giving, with every perfect gift, is from above, coming down from the Father of lights, with whom there is no variation or shadow due to change" (Jas 1:17). That was Vera's faith, and it was Calvin's. Their lives have schooled me in the ways of God and of the soul.

In regeneration we become creatures of God, free to be just that. As Dietrich Bonhoeffer wrote, "The real man is at liberty to be his Creator's creature."[4] The more truly human we become, the more we become like Christ, the true human, the true image of God. We become the image of God not by any attempt of ours to become divine, but by God's work to make us human.

Twelve

The Shape of
Peace Is Love

••••••••••••••••••••••••••••••••••••••

*I*n our dying and rising with Christ the works of the flesh are cut off, while our life in the Spirit sets heavy with the fruit of the Spirit. Jesus told his disciples on the night he was betrayed, "I am the vine, you are the branches. Those who abide in me and I in them bear much fruit, because apart from me you can do nothing" (Jn 15:5). What is the fruit we produce? The fruit of the Spirit of Jesus is love: "I appointed you to go and bear fruit, fruit that will last. . . . I am giving you these commands so that you may love one another" (Jn 15:16-17).

Paul says much the same thing when he tells the Galatian Christians, "By contrast, the fruit of the Spirit is love, joy, peace, patience, kindness, generosity, faithfulness, gentleness, and self-control" (Gal 5:22-23).

The flesh works a hideous independence from the Spirit; walking in the Spirit produces the fruit of the Spirit. The Spirit-genetic makeup of the regenerate soul produces the fruit of peace with the shape, color and taste of love. Peace is the fruit of God's love, and his love produces peace in our lives.

We enjoy our peace in Christ. Paul shows us how God's peace takes the form of love:

> Therefore, since we are justified by faith, we have peace with God through our Lord Jesus Christ, through whom we have obtained access to this grace in which we stand; and we boast in our hope of sharing the glory of God. And not only that, but we also boast in our sufferings, knowing that suffering produces endurance, and endurance produces character, and character produces hope, and hope does not disappoint us, because God's love has been poured into our hearts through the Holy Spirit that has been given to us. (Rom 5:1-5)

We Have Peace with God

God's love incarnate for us in Jesus Christ creates the peace of reconciliation. God ended our soul's war with him in Christ. He served justice, defeated death and began the process of making his peace take shape in our lives.

Reconciliation is the precondition *and* the experience of peace. The experience of peace must be preceded by the covenant that ends hostility. Christ establishes the *terms* of our covenant reconciliation with God, and he initiates the *process* of our relational reconciliation with God.

The terms of reconciliation are the covenant of peace purchased with Jesus' blood. Our personal experience of peace with God is based on an act of justice by God, not on a particular theology about God's attributes. It is well and good to be the proud owner of a theology of a loving God. But in the clinch, when our sense of sin and guilt has overwhelmed our cognition—as ICU units and the like are wont to do—it is the act of God, not a thought about God, that gives us peace.

As a pastor I thank God for the crucifixes found in the rooms of Catholic hospitals. Similarly, persons in deep sin are often healed by the Lord's Supper, a concrete demonstration of the death of Christ for sin, more than by all the kind, encouraging words any of us can muster.

Relational reconciliation is prayer. What was previously a prayer-as-needed relationship grows into a life of prayer. Such peace is not so much praying for things and getting answers—many non-Christians pray and receive answers to their prayers—as it is the Holy Spirit within our souls crying out the prayer of the Son of God to the Father. We gain a fresh consciousness that God is with us and in us always. Prayer becomes less a series of specially designed sentences directed to God than an open, constant awareness that God is listening to all we say and think, constantly interacting with us in innumerable ways. He is simply *always there.*

But: relational peace with God is dependent ever and again on the constant reminder and reestablishment of the terms of reconciliation. Sin and guilt really do get in the way of the awareness of God's presence.

The Lord's Supper does wonders for our prayer lives, as does gospel preaching. One good sermon on the love of God and the forgiveness of God established in the cross often does more for prayer than a hundred sermons on how to pray, many of which create feelings of guilt—precisely in the people who pray the most.

Reconciliation with God reconciles us with one another and with all creation. Such reconciliation takes time: to say this is to acknowledge the historical nature of our lives, our shared life as humans, and our shared life with all creation. Our reconciliation with one another comes from our reconciliation with God. Reconciliation with one another on a personal, relational level requires forgiveness of one another. Our forgiveness for one another comes from God's forgiveness of us in Christ. Denying ourselves the privilege to forgive and be reconciled leads to incredible loss for us, as Jesus says, "For if you forgive others their trespasses, your heavenly Father will also forgive you; but if you do not forgive others, neither will your Father forgive your trespasses" (Mt 6:14-15).

Reconciliation with God and all humanity and all creation is our great peace and our great hope. The book of Revelation gives us glimpses of the great reconciliation: "After this I looked, and there was a great multitude that no one could count, from every nation, from all tribes and peoples and languages, standing before the throne and before the Lamb, robed in white, with palm branches in their hands" (Rev 7:9).

The peace of reconciliation, certain in the future, lives in our souls now as hope. Hope does not dwell in the soul easily. The soul learns to hope in and through the experience of God's loving care through life's joys and sorrows. This makes us people of character.

We Boast in Our Sufferings

God's love working in his providential care creates the peace of character. God's providential hand guides us, protects us, corrects us and encourages us throughout our lives. David was the great poet of providence.

O LORD, you have searched me and known me.
You know when I sit down and when I rise up;
    you discern my thoughts from far away.
You search out my path and my lying down,
    and are acquainted with all my ways.
Even before a word is on my tongue,
    O LORD, you know it completely.
You hem me in, behind and before,
    and lay your hand upon me. . . .
My frame was not hidden from you,
    when I was being made in secret,
    intricately woven in the depths of the earth.
Your eyes beheld my unformed substance.
In your book were written
    all the days that were formed for me,
    when none of them as yet existed. (Ps 139:1-5, 15-16)

God's providence is an objective reality: we can see in the past how he has intervened on our behalf, and we trust our future in his hand. God's providence is also a subjective reality: knowing that God leads us beside still waters, that he is with us in the valley of the shadow of death, that he is acquainted with all our ways, leads to the personal experience of his presence and his peace. In the midst of our chaotic existence, his Spirit still hovers over the deep things of our lives. "Deep calleth unto deep at the noise of thy waterspouts: all thy waves and thy billows are gone over me" (Ps 42:7 KJV).

The experience of God's peace is not a matter of mysticism as much as a matter of character. True mysticism follows true character. Seeking the mystical touch without paying the price for character is the basis of witchcraft. Witchcraft, the original religious technology, tries to handle power without holiness, to secure life without integrity. However, holding power and securing life are two different things.

At the end of a century and a half of unparalleled technological advancement, we blithely handle more and more technological power, and we have become less and less convinced of God's providential care of our lives. Is it because we think we have taken control of so many things that at one time we thought were under God's direct hand? Or is it because as we have fouled the air, poisoned the rivers, killed millions and lost control of our families, we blame God for letting us cause all this trouble?

In the face of the problem of evil we succor ourselves by calling our accusations of God courage, but our fist-raising has decreased our character. Lacking character, we lack the strength to grasp hope. Without hope we cannot experience God's presence in our lives, and without that we have no life.

Rather than curse our sufferings, we learn to boast in them. "For the Lord disciplines those whom he loves, and chastises every child whom he accepts" (Heb 12:6). Character is precious to those who obtain it; the benefits are enormous and the cost is dear. Furthermore, I never knew a soul of true character, cleaving to genuine hope, producing enduring peace, that begrudged God the cost.

God's Love Has Been Poured into Our Hearts

God's love poured into us creates the peace of meaning. What is better than to have meaningful work? What is better than to look back on a significant accomplishment? What is better than to consider commendable goals? The soul revels in life that matters, the expenditure of energy directed with meaning in the creation of beauty, goodness, truth and holiness. The greatest of these is love: the beauty of love, the goodness of love, truth in love, and the burning fire of holy love. The Holy Spirit pours love into our hearts, love that demands action for satisfaction and that creates satisfaction in completion. Peace issues from work energized by love.

Work energized by pride and self-love entrenches our isolation. Self-love is centripetal. It gathers energy as it spins in and down, not unlike the flushing of a toilet. Its energy source is gravity. The human soul is meant to be full, empty, light and breathing; the centripetal force of self-love, however, compacts the soul and eventually crushes it. Peace does not come from love directed toward the soul.

Holy Spirit love is centrifugal. The energy source is outside the soul, but it applies itself precisely from the center of the soul. The more Christ is at the center of the soul, the more balanced the spin. Whereas the centripetal force of self-love gathers energy into the center, the centrifugal force of Holy Spirit love expends energy outside the self. "But you will receive power when the Holy Spirit has come upon you; and you will be my witnesses in Jerusalem, in all Judea and Samaria, and to the ends of the earth" (Acts 1:8).

When our love for one another is Holy Spirit love, forcing itself outward from the center of our soul, the recipient of this grace experiences human love and divine love from the person of the human lover and the person of the divine lover. Jesus tells us, "Whoever welcomes you welcomes me, and whoever welcomes me welcomes the one who sent me" (Mt 10:40). This love draws the beloved into the life and fellowship of the body of Jesus. As we love one another, we are drawn together into the life of God: "I in them and you in me, that they may become completely one" (Jn 17:23).

Quiet time comes when the Spirit reverses love's outward

inertia, allowing us to be in stillness. Energy, rather than gathering inward or pushing outward, is expended within as divine-human knowing. By the Spirit the soul is enabled to experience God's love from within, Spirit to spirit, Word of existence to word of existence, a brief taste of heaven's "face to face."

That we experience this peace so infrequently is due either to our attempts to mimic the experience with a religious-technical meditation that becomes nothing more than centripetal self-love or to the way we keep our motor running and our wheels spinning by our own power, doing good ad nauseam, believing that peace comes when we deserve it. Peace is grace. To experience this peace we need to listen for the Spirit's gentle insistence to stop working and begin feeling the love of God present within.

In this peace, at times, God enables us to read the history of what we have accomplished: in the Spirit, in a sense, it seems, right out of the Book of Life. When we read this Book, the question who produced the fruit of love, God or us, is moot.

We Boast in Our Hope of Sharing the Glory of God

God's love in our future creates the peace of hope. With nothing but the greatest mercy in mind, Jesus tells us, "In this world you will have trouble. But take heart! I have overcome the world" (Jn 16:33 NIV).

Jesus grants us the mercy to understand ahead of time that having trouble is a norm for life in this world. We live our little lives in the course of the great river of all human life. Even as tiny subcurrents, we each belong to the same great river. We are flowing in this life in the same direction, and we experience weal and woe along the course together with our fellow human beings. To deny this is to deny our humanness and our belonging to humanity.

The denial of our complicity in the woe of the world in which we live is at least one source of the enduring power of gnosticism. It is not merely wanting to rise to life before we die—though it is most certainly that—it is believing that we *deserve* to rise before we die, believing that the divine reality at work in us makes us something other than human beings and grants us special privileges.

Jesus, on the other hand, overcame the world in his death as much as in his resurrection. Our participation in his death and resurrection calls for our life and our death in and with the world, even though we are resurrected out of the world of death into a world of life. So yes, in this world we will have trouble.

But Jesus *has* overcome the world. And though we live and die in a world in which "in toil you shall eat of it all the days of your life; thorns and thistles it shall bring forth for you" (Gen 3:17-18), there exists for humanity a new Adam, a new progenitor, leading us into our original destiny, into the Garden of Life, an eternal sabbath rest of peace in and with all creation in God.

This peace exists as God's absolute future. Absolute future extends its power in every direction, touching us now. The peace of God's absolute future is a deliciously paradoxical presence of resurrection in the face of—not in denial of—the world of trouble we live in now, and it fills the soul with hope and boasting. The world despises our hope and our boasting. Our hope is an audacious cheer of victory before the game appears to be won.

The Death of Boredom

Peace is the destruction of boredom. Boredom is having nothing to do, nothing to see, nothing to feel, nothing to taste. It is either the absence of beauty, goodness, truth, and holiness or the inability or unwillingness to know and create these realities in our lives. Hell is all three: absence, inability and unwillingness. For some, the transition from life to death is already occurring. Without the intervention of the regeneration of God, their souls continue to degenerate until there is little difference between life here and death there.

Boredom is, perhaps more than any disease in our world, a disease of the soul. Though we think of it as physical deprivation—for example, the boredom of lying in a hospital bed—often people possessing vast material advantages are very bored. Boredom isn't nothing to do on the outside, it is nothing happening on the inside. Boredom is the symptom of a starved soul.

Some souls really are deprived. They live in flat, gray environments, worlds without beauty, goodness, truth and holiness. Other souls are unable to take nourishment. They are surrounded by goodness, but they are unable to metabolize it. Some souls simply refuse to know anything outside of themselves.

The idea that our souls are by nature full of beauty, goodness, truth and holiness and that we can live on these resources within is the source of endless foolishness and timeless boredom. "There is no one who has understanding, there is no one who seeks God. All have turned aside, together they have become worthless; there is no one who shows kindness, there is not even one" (Rom 3:11-12). These are lives of utter boredom. Boredom is the mother of cynicism.

The only Bible character who seems to have been truly bored was Solomon.

I said to myself, "Come now, I will make a test of pleasure; enjoy yourself." But again, this also was vanity. I said of laughter, "It is mad," and of pleasure, "What use is it?" I searched with my mind how to cheer my body with wine—my mind still guiding me with wisdom—and how to lay hold on folly, until I might see what was good for mortals to do under heaven during the few days of their life. I made great works; I built houses and planted vineyards for myself; I made myself gardens and parks, and planted in them all kinds of fruit trees. I made myself pools from which to water the forest of growing trees. I bought male and female slaves, and had slaves who were born in my house; I also had great possessions of herds and flocks, more than any who had been before me in Jerusalem. I also gathered for myself silver and gold and the treasure of kings and of the provinces; I got singers, both men and women, and delights of the flesh, and many concubines.

So I became great and surpassed all who were before me in Jerusalem; also my wisdom remained with me. Whatever my eyes desired I did not keep from them; I kept my heart from no pleasure, for my heart found pleasure in all my toil, and this was my reward for all my toil. Then I considered all that my hands had done and the toil I had spent in doing it, and again, all was vanity and a chasing after wind, and there was nothing to be gained under the sun. (Eccles 2:1-11)

The first-century Roman world was marked by popular boredom and cynicism. Paul's realistic analysis of the situation was "If the dead are not raised, 'Let us eat and drink, for tomorrow we die' " (1 Cor 15:32). Eating and drinking, alternating between self-stimulation and a self-anesthesia leading to slow death, are typical of boredom. The process is typical of bodies unstimulated from within, bodies without throbbing, vital souls, bodies and souls dis-integrating.

The separation of the body and the soul is the definition of death. Boredom is the symptom of the beginning of this process in our lives. It points to the separation of body and soul and leads to behavior that furthers the separation.

Glory

Peace, the taking shape of God's love in our lives, is integrative. Peace is the experience of the soul's generation by God's love, which then generates a whole human life—body and soul—of love. Our hope for peace lies in the total integration of body and soul: souls in bodies that cannot die, bodies with souls that cannot sin, living in heavens and worlds of glorious radiance, creative possibilities and direct knowing, face to face with God.

John saw this world ahead of us. He glimpsed it, and wrote about it for our spiritual digestion, for the sanctification of our imaginations. In the new world boredom is vanquished.

Then I saw a new heaven and a new earth; for the first heaven and the first earth had passed away, and the sea was no more. And I saw the holy city, the new Jerusalem, coming down out of heaven from God, prepared as a bride adorned for her husband. And I heard a loud voice from the throne saying,

"See, the home of God is among mortals.
He will dwell with them as their God;
they will be his peoples,

and God himself will be with them;
he will wipe every tear from their eyes.
Death will be no more;
mourning and crying and pain will be no more,
for the first things have passed away." (Rev 21:1-4)

God's absolute future touches us now in sanctified words and sanctified deeds. Many times I have read this passage at funeral services through tears. From Word we process to sacrament, to food prepared in love. We gather as brothers and sisters in the fellowship hall to consume Jell-O salad, love salad, a shimmering, sweet, cool gift-from-hands-that-love salad, whose mission is to bring peace to a time of pain. The love affirms the past, the sweetness on the tongue confirms the present, the tickling down the throat points to our future together of transparent, colorful laughter.

Notes

Introduction

[1]Bruce Waltke, "Nephesh," in *Theological Wordbook of the Old Testament*, edited by Bruce Waltke (Chicago: Moody Press, 1980), p. 590.

[2]Ibid.

[3]David Noel Freedman, ed., *The Anchor Bible Dictionary* (New York: Doubleday, 1992). *The Anchor Bible Dictionary* contains a short article on "the preexistence of souls," but nothing on the soul specifically. This is very odd, since the biblical doctrine of the soul is a matter of traditional, historical exegesis of no little importance. Likewise, and one must admit consistently, *The Anchor Bible Dictionary* contains no article on the human spirit or the heart.

Chapter 1: The Soul Is What Goes to Heaven

[1]Karl Barth, *Church Dogmatics* 3/2, *The Doctrine of Creation*, edited by G. W. Bromiley and T. F. Torrance (Edinburgh: T & T Clark, 1960), p. 334: "When Jesus sighs or is moved or angered or troubled in spirit, when He commends His spirit into the hands of God (Luke 23:46), and when He gives up the spirit (Mt 27:50, Jn 19:30), the word 'spirit' is used in a general anthropological sense for the word 'soul' and does not refer at all (or only indirectly) to the Holy Spirit."

[2]I. Howard Marshall, *The Gospel of Luke: A Commentary on the Greek Text* (Grand Rapids, Mich.: Eerdmans, 1978), p. 873.

[3]Ibid., p. 872.

Chapter 2: The Soul Is Empty

[1]"The demonic power of idolatry lies in its deceitful persuasion which insists that we already believe"—Alan Poole.

[2]Hans Walter Wolff, *Anthropology of the Old Testament*, trans. Margaret Kohl (Philadelphia: Fortress, 1974), p. 10.

[3]Ibid., pp. 11-15.

[4]Ibid., p. 15. (The italics are Wolff's.)

[5]Karl Barth, *Church Dogmatics* 3/2, *The Doctrine of Creation*, edited by G. W. Bromiley and T. F. Torrance (Edinburgh: T & T Clark, 1960), p. 353.

[6]Samuel Rutherford, *Letters of Samuel Rutherford* (Carlisle, Penn.: Banner of Truth Trust, 1984), p. 169.

[7]Barth, *Church Dogmatics* 3/2, p. 344.

[8]C. F. D. Moule, *The Phenomenon of the New Testament* (London: SCM Press, 1967), p. 26.

[9]Ibid., p. 27.

[10]John W. Cooper, *Body, Soul and Life Everlasting* (Grand Rapids, Mich.: Eerdmans, 1989), p. 9.

[11]Barth, *Church Dogmatics* 3/2, p. 355.

[12]Wolff, *Anthropology of the Old Testament*, p. 7.

[13]Ibid., p. 8.

Chapter 3: Fuel, Air & Spark

[1]Hans Walter Wolff, *Anthropology of the Old Testament*, trans. Margaret Kohl (Philadelphia: Fortress, 1974), p. 40.

[2]Ibid.

[3]Ibid.

[4]Karl Barth, *Church Dogmatics* 3/2, *The Doctrine of Creation*, ed. G. W. Bromiley and T. F. Torrance (Edinburgh: T & T Clark, 1960), p. 540.

[5]David Hansen, *The Art of Pastoring: Ministry Without All the Answers* (Downers Grove, Ill.: InterVarsity Press, 1994), pp. 125-26.

[6]Ibid., p. 126.

[7]I am quite sure that pastors' *wives* are subject to these forces. I don't know enough about the lives of pastors' *husbands* to suggest that they suffer similarly.

[8]Sin is a soul issue. A sane person can be a great sinner and an insane person a dear saint. Some of the sanest people in the world find the cleverest ways to rebel against God with the freest choice. Mentally ill people don't have as much choice as to the direction their rebellion against God will take. The characteristics of the unconscious may channel sin this way or that, but the root of sin itself, rebellion against God, goes to the heart of the soul, as we shall discuss later.

[9]As interesting and helpful as it might be to discuss the issue of demon possession further here, such a discussion goes beyond the scope of this book.

Chapter 4: Self-Portrait in Ice Water

[1]Animals have the breath of life *(nishmath-ruach chayyah):* see Genesis 7:22. Animals are "living beings" *(nephesh chayyah):* Genesis 1:21, 24; 2:19; and especially 9:10, 12, where the Lord makes the covenant of the rainbow with Noah, his descendants and all "living beings," meaning all animals.

[2]Karl Barth, *Church Dogmatics* 3/2, *The Doctrine of Creation*, edited by G. W. Bromiley and T. F. Torrance (Edinburgh: T & T Clark, 1960), p. 361. See also Wolfhart Pannenberg, *Systematic Theology* (Grand Rapids, Mich.: Eerdmans, 1994), 2:189.

[3]C. S. Lewis, *The Four Loves* (New York: Harcourt Brace Jovanovich, 1960), p. 53.

[4]George MacDonald, *Getting to Know Jesus* (New Canaan, Conn.: Kents, 1980), p. 34.

[5]Nahum Sarna, *Exploring Exodus* (New York: Schocken, 1986), p. 52.

[6]Roland de Vaux, *The Early History of Israel* (Philadelphia: Westminster Press, 1978), p. 354.

[7]Gerhard von Rad, *Old Testament Theology*, trans. D. M. G. Stalker (New York: Harper & Row, 1962), 1:185.

[8]Sarna, *Exploring Exodus*, p. 52.

[9]"It is of course true that nothing is more impressive and palpable than our being in the present. How many skeptics have thought they could take refuge in the boast 'I am'! And what structures of assurance have been erected on the foundation of this boast!" (Barth, *Church Dogmatics* 3/2, p. 528).

[10]"Man can be human without God. There is no doubt that man can do that. He can live without experiencing God. He can speak, hear, think, and act without speaking about God, without perceiving God, without thinking of God, without working for him. And he can do that all very well and with great responsibility" (Eberhard Jüngel, *God as the Mystery of the World*, trans. Darrell L. Guder [Grand Rapids, Mich.: Eerdmans, 1983], p. 20).

Chapter 5: Beauty

[1]Patrick Sherry, *Spirit and Beauty* (Oxford: Clarendon, 1992), p. 134.

[2]Ibid.

[3]Ibid.

[4]Ibid., p. 135.

[5]Ibid.

[6]Ibid.

[7]Ibid.

Chapter 9: War Against God

[1]Wendell Berry, "The Gift of Good Land," in *The Gift of Good Land: Further Essays Cultural and Agricultural* (San Francisco: North Point, 1981), pp. 267-81.

[2]Wendell Berry, "Christianity and the Survival of Creation," in *Sex, Economy, Freedom and Community* (New York: Pantheon, 1992), p. 104.

[3]Wendell Berry, "Health Is Membership," in *Another Turn of the Crank* (Washington, D.C.: Counterpoint, 1995), pp. 90, 93.

[4]Berry, "Christianity and the Survival," pp. 105, 107.

[5]Berry, "Health Is Membership," p. 91.

[6]Ibid., p. 90.

[7]Ibid., p. 91.

[8]Ibid., p. 89.

[9]Berry, "The Conservation and Nature of the Preservation of Humanity," in *Another Turn of the Crank* (Washington, D.C.: Counterpoint, 1995), p. 67.

[10]Berry, "Christianity and the Survival," p. 109.

[11]Kurt Rudolph, *Gnosis*, trans. Robert McLachlan Wilson (San Francisco: Harper & Row, 1987), p. 60.

[12] J. N. D. Kelly, *Early Christian Doctrines* (San Francisco: Harper & Row, 1960), p. 26.

[13] Ibid.

[14] Ibid., p. 27.

Chapter 10: Overreligion

[1] Leonhard Goppelt, *Theology of the New Testament*, trans. John E. Alsup, ed. Jürgen Roloff (Grand Rapids, Mich.: Eerdmans, 1981), 1:26.

[2] Kai Erikson, *Wayward Puritans: A Study in the Sociology of Deviance* (New York: John Wiley & Sons, 1966) p. 13.

[3] Ernst Käsemann, *Perspectives on Paul*, trans. Margaret Kohl (Philadelphia: Fortress, 1971), p. 35.

[4] The Apostle's Creed tells us "he descended into hell." For the history of this much-debated sentence see Philip Schaff, *The Creeds of Christendom*, 6th ed. (Grand Rapids, Mich.: Baker Book House, 1977), 2:46.

[5] Martin Luther, "The Freedom of the Christian," in *Three Treatises*, trans. W. L. Lambert, rev. Harold J. Grimm (Philadelphia: Fortress, 1970), p. 286.

Chapter 11: Dying & Rising with Christ

[1] Rudolf Schnackenburg, "Dying and Rising with Christ," in *Present and Future*, trans. Denis Burkhard and Michael Steinhauser (Notre Dame, Ind.: Notre Dame University Press, 1966), p. 115.

[2] Ephesians, Philippians, Colossians and Philemon.

[3] *New International Version* (Grand Rapids, Mich.: Zondervan Bible Publishers, 1978), p. viii.

[4] Dietrich Bonhoeffer, *Ethics*, ed. Eberhard Bethge, trans. Neville Horton Smith (New York: Macmillan, 1955), p. 8.